# THE **REALLY, REALLY, REALLY** STEP-BY-STEP GUIDE TO BUILDING YOUR OWN WEBSITE

## for absolute beginners of all ages

D0825720

Gavin Hoole and Cheryl Smith

NH
NEW HOLLAND

# Contents

SHATFORD LIBRARY

APR     2010

1570 E. Colorado Blvd.
Pasadena. CA 91106

# Read this before you start

## IT'S EASY!

Developing a website is not nearly as difficult as many people believe it to be. In fact, it's pretty easy. It's just that many people don't yet know how to go about it, or what's involved, how it all works, where to start, who to talk to, and so on. This book will take the mystery out of website building and get you up and running quickly with your own website that you will have created yourself from scratch. You won't need a graphic artist, and you won't need a computer expert to blind you with computer science and buzzwords. By following this book's really, really, really easy step-by-step processes, written in user-friendly language, you'll find the whole journey quite a breeze.

## ADVANTAGES OF THE DIY APPROACH

Besides the fun of being able to create your own website, the do-it-yourself approach also has several other important advantages over using a professional Web design service. Here are a few of them.

- Obviously, you can save yourself a fair amount of time and money, especially if your site is going to need ongoing periodic updates.

- You'll avoid any frustration associated with having to work through someone else, and with perhaps having to tell them that what they've created is actually not quite what you had in mind – leading to more design fees and delays.

- Once your website is up on the World Wide Web you'll probably find that you'll need to make some changes, particularly during the development stages when you're still adding new pages and tweaking information and layouts here and there. Instead of having to wait until your commercial Webmaster can schedule the job for you for an additional fee, you can make those changes yourself – there and then, within minutes – and do it at any hour of the day or night. This is a real boon later on as well, when you have something new and important that you want to get up onto your website in a hurry.

In short, you become empowered to manage your own Internet presence the way you want to, when you want to, and at a cost that suits your budget.

 **MICROSOFT WINDOWS XP HAS BEEN USED FOR THIS BOOK** This book assumes that you will have easy access to a computer as well as an Internet connection. The screenshots and procedures given are based on the Microsoft Windows XP operating system. If you are using some other operating system you will need to make adaptations accordingly when you work through the step-by-step procedures and refer to the accompanying screenshots.

## THE USER-FRIENDLY VISUAL SYSTEM

The same user-friendly visual system as used in all the books in this series makes it really, really, really easy for you to enjoy developing your own website.

Colour coded text windows are used throughout the book so that you can see at a glance the type of information you're looking at:

- introductions and explanations in normal black text on a white background;

- step-by-step action procedures in yellow boxes;

- hints and tips in blue boxes;

- very important notes and warnings in boxes with red borders;

- supportive explanatory information in grey panels.

Where necessary, the detailed procedures are supported by illustrations to make learning easier.

 **WORK YOUR WAY THROUGH EACH CHAPTER IN SEQUENCE** This step-by-step workbook is designed to be used chapter-by-chapter. Working through it in its proper sequence will help you do 'first things first' and learn the correct ways of tackling the various processes and methodologies that follow in subsequent chapters. You'll first have the opportunity to build a practice website with us. Then, based on your hands-on experience, you'll follow the same procedures to build your own website: from planning, creating and testing, right through to publishing it on the World Wide Web.

### TIP: THIS BOOK HAS A COMPANION WEBSITE

At our website you can download free Web page design software, as well as a program you'll need for getting your website into the public domain for viewing by everyone worldwide. The site also has hyperlinks to a number of useful website development sites for learning more about this subject. The address (URL) for the home page of our website is:

http://www.reallyeasycomputerbooks.com

**Let's have some fun!**

# 1 Laying the foundations

Before getting into the step-by-step processes of building a website, it will be useful to have a basic understanding of what a website is, how it's made up and how it works.

## THE ANATOMY OF A WEBSITE

**Web pages:** Individual pages are the building blocks of every website. They consist of text and graphics, and perhaps a few other components – like the many Web pages you've no doubt already visited. Each Web page is a separate file that has been created in a suitable program designed for the job. And each graphic (photo or other image) is likewise a separate file. In this book we'll take you through the easy step-by-step processes of designing your own Web pages and adding images to them.

Individual page files, with images – the building blocks of a website

Each completed Web page and each image is saved as a separate file in a folder on your computer, just as you would save any other file. These individual files then become your 'website imminent', or offline website. Because these files are still stored only on your own computer, your Web pages are obviously not yet accessible to Internet users worldwide. To make them available for others to view, you need to have them stored on a computer that is connected to the Internet 24 hours a day, every day of the year, and which is accessible to anyone, anywhere, who has Internet access. Such a hosting computer is known as a *Web server* – it 'serves' a particular Web page to any computer that requests to view it in its Web browser software, such as Internet Explorer, Firefox or Opera.

**Web server:** A Web server normally has a very large disk capacity in order to store a huge number of Web page files for the many individuals, companies and organizations whose websites are hosted on that server. Web server space is typically offered by the Internet Service Provider who provides your Internet access (dial-up or broadband) and by other companies that specialize in providing such hosting services. Some individuals may act as agents for Web hosting companies, and sometimes they portray themselves as being the business that is actually 'offering' the service.

The hosting Web servers could be anywhere in the world, not necessarily in your home country. Transferring your Web pages from your hard drive onto such a Web server is called uploading and is done via an Internet connection using a process known as File Transfer Protocol (ftp). In this book we'll show you how easy it is to upload your own completed website files to your hosting Web server.

| Website files are uploaded by you from your hard disk, for storing on the hosting server's disk | The hosting server 'serves' those files to requesting computers 24/7, for viewing in their browsers (e.g. Internet Explorer) | Requesting computers download the files for display as Web pages in their Web browsers |

**Website address:** Once your Web pages have been uploaded to a Web server, you have a functional website that anyone can visit from anywhere in the world. However, for people to be able to find your website, they'll need to know which of the thousands of Internet-connected Web servers around the world is storing your files – that is, they'll need the unique address for locating your particular website's *home page*. Such an address is known as a *Universal Resource Locator* (*URL* – an abbreviation worth remembering, as it is used often in Internet jargon).

**Domain name:** There are many hosting services available on the Internet that offer free Web space. However, the URL that you have to use with a free hosting service is often quite long and something like http://www.reallyeasycomputerbooks.com/members/poolservices.html.

This is a pretty cumbersome website URL and not an easy one to remember or to fit on a business card. It's certainly not a very appropriate URL if you wish to portray a professional image for your business, club, family or community website. Many website owners therefore prefer to have a URL that shows their own business or family name directly after the 'http://www'. In other words, they want to own their own domain name, so that a business by the name of Pool Services could have a neater website URL such as http://www.poolservices.com. Such a domain is not expensive to register.

**Getting visitors to your site ('traffic' or 'hits'):** There's no point in spending time developing a website if no one knows about it. This brings us to the very important aspect of getting traffic to your site. Most people find and visit websites via *search engines* such as Google, Yahoo!, MSN and AOL. Getting more visitors to (or 'hits' on) your site via search engines is done through a process called Search Engine Optimization (SEO for short), which can be quite intimidating for a beginner. However, we've distilled it all down to a few important yet simple things you can do to increase your chances of getting a fair share of Internet traffic to your site. Many people are surprised to learn that search engine optimization actually starts *before* you begin designing your Web pages. This will be explained in the next chapter about planning your site.

**Web Counters:** What country do your visitors come from? How many hits does your site get every day, week, month or year? Which of your content pages gets the most visitors? Which search engines do your visitors use most often, and – importantly – what keywords do they enter into their searches? These are questions you should know the answers to. There are many websites offering free counters, and some of these are included in our online list of useful websites for beginner Webmasters. Visit us at:

### http://www.reallyeasycomputerbooks.com

**Site architecture:** A successful site is one that has been well designed for ease of navigation, with pages that load quickly, and that provides the kind of useful information your target audience is looking for. It all starts with thoughtful planning before you even begin creating your Web pages.

As we move through each step in the process of building a website from scratch, we'll go into more detail about each of these important elements of a good website. You'll learn exactly what you need to do in order to become the proud owner and Webmaster of your own self-created piece of 'real estate' on the World Wide Web.

---

**!** **OVERVIEW OF THE TUTORIAL PROCESS** Here is the process you'll be following in this book's tutorials:

- **Learn how to plan your website from scratch.**
- **Work with us in building a <u>practice website</u> to gain hands-on experience in building a real, working website on your computer before you tackle the project of building your own site.**
- **Refer to our own fully-functional <u>demo website</u> (which you'll have on your hard drive) to compare your practice site with our completed demo site and make any adjustments, if necessary, to get yours to match the demo site.**
- **Use this knowledge and hands-on experience to start planning and building your own site.**
- **Once you've completed your own site, you'll follow our remaining tutorials to find a hosting service, have your domain name registered and upload your files to the remote hosting server.**

  **In order to achieve all of this, you'll first need to download the free tools.**

---

## DOWNLOAD THE FREE TOOLS YOU'LL NEED

You'll need some Web design software and other useful aids to help you develop your website. You can download some of these free items at our website and the others can be obtained from our website's links to external software sites. Here's a list of the items you should download, all available free of charge:

- **Good Keywords** – software for finding the best high-demand keywords to use for your particular site (an essential part of search engine optimization).

- **Keyword Explorer** – software for establishing the extent of competition (other websites) that already contain those same keywords you're considering using, so that you can hone your site with good keywords that are used in a lot in searches but for which there are not millions of competing websites. In this way you'll increase your likelihood of attracting your share of traffic.

- **PageBreeze** – Web authoring and design software you'll be using as you follow the step-by-step procedures to create a practice website with us, and then to build your own website.

- **FTP Commander** – a program for uploading your Web pages to the Web server.

- **Irfanview** – a photo editing program for cropping and resizing images.

- **Adobe Reader** – for reading PDF (Portable Document File) pages (you only need to download this if you don't already have a PDF reader installed on your computer)

- **A demo website** – a complete, fully functional website – including images – for you to have on your hard drive, so that you can refer to it while you build the practice website with us.

- **Various documents and worksheets (optional)** – e.g. instructions for downloading and installing the various programs (for those who may not be familiar with this task); plus some optional aids to help you when planning your own website's concept, structure and page content.

Here's a checklist you can use to make sure you've downloaded all the essential files from the links named as follows on our website:

> ❑ WebsiteTools.exe (this file *must* be downloaded to the **My Webs** folder in My Documents)
> ❑ PageBreeze
> ❑ Irfanview
> ❑ Adobe Reader (if not already installed on your computer)

**DOWNLOAD WEBSITE TOOLS.EXE TO THE 'MY WEBS' FOLDER** For the tutorials that follow, it is <u>essential</u> that you download the file named *WebsiteTools.exe* to the *My Webs* folder, which is in *My Documents*. If your computer doesn't have a *My Webs* folder, here's how to create one.

## To create a My Webs folder in My Documents (if one does not already exist)

1  In My Computer or Windows Explorer, click on the **My Documents** folder to select it.
2  On the Menu bar, click on **File > New ▸ Folder**.
3  In the little **New Folder** box that appears at the end of any other folders you may have in My Documents, type the name **My Webs** and press ⏎ .

## Download the WebsiteTools.exe file first

1  Open your Web browser (e.g. Internet Explorer, Firefox, Netscape, Opera) and go to our companion website at **http://www.reallyeasycomputerbooks.com**.
2  Once you've entered the website via the home page, click on the link: **Website Building**.
3  On the page that opens, click on the link named **Downloads**.
4  In the Downloads page that opens, click on the link **WebsiteTools.exe** to download that file. (The dialog box that then opens will depend on the browser software you're using, and may offer the option to Run the file. <u>Choose the **Save** option, not Run</u>.)
5  Click on **Save** to save the file to the **My Webs** folder in My Documents.
6  Once it's been downloaded, use My Computer or Windows Explorer to browse to and open My Webs, and double-click on the file named **WebsiteTools.exe**; its contents will then be extracted automatically to their correct sub-folders within My Webs.

When done, you should see the folders in My Webs as shown here on the right.

Now that the folders and files have been extracted, the ZIP folder *WebsiteTools.exe* will no longer be needed and should be deleted.

1  Click on **WebsiteTools.exe** to select it.
2  Press Del on your keyboard to delete the file.

## Download the other programs next

There are three other free programs you'll need. They are all available from websites that can be accessed from our website's Downloads page.

1 Back at our website's Downloads page, click on the first program in the list (**PageBreeze**), and you'll be taken to the website that offers that particular program.

2 Follow the links at that independent site until you get to the download link for the program; then click on it to commence the download.

3 For each program you download, select the **Save** option and save it to your **Downloads** folder, or the folder you usually use for downloading software from the Internet.

4 If you need additional guidance on how to download and install these programs, click on the link **Downloading and installing guidelines** link on our website.

5 Repeat these steps for the other programs in the list on page 9, and tick each one off once it's been downloaded.

## THE NEXT STEP

Once you have all the key resources you'll need for developing your website, the next step will be to start planning the site itself.

# 2 Planning your site

**PLAN YOUR SITE** Before you do anything else, take a step back to do some critically important website development planning. Do not allow impatience to cause you to leap ahead and skip this part of the process. The steps that follow in this chapter, and the next, are all vital if you want to develop a good site that brings in the visitors you're looking for.

## DETERMINE YOUR SITE CONCEPT AND GOALS

The first stage in the planning process is to clarify what kind of site you want to build. Your entire site structure will then be geared to supporting your site's concept and goals.

### WHAT'S A SITE CONCEPT?

A site concept is the overall theme and purpose of the particular website. Here are some examples: a **commercial** site to promote your products or services; a **club** site to give information about your club and its activities, the events calendar, membership application details and the like; a **family** site to share family news with friends and relatives locally or abroad; a **religious organization's** site giving information about your religious organization (church, etc.), perhaps past sermons, articles and so on; an **inspirational** site offering articles, quotations and personal growth advice, with links to other similar sites; a **resources** site giving information on a subject or theme that interests you, with links to many other sites that people with the same interests as yours might find useful.

### Define your site's main concept and intended content

Once you've clarified the kind of site you wish to build, specify (broadly) your main concept or theme and the kind of content you plan to have on your site – i.e. the topics your individual pages will cover. For example, if you're building a site to promote your wood furniture restoration business, your main theme and content might be specified as follows:

**Core site concept (example):** To let people in my local community know that I offer a very specialized service relating to wood furniture restoration and repair.

**Theme-related topics (initial list):**
- Wood furniture restoration, refinishing and re-creation
- Antique and contemporary wood furniture
- Large wood pieces to small treasures
- Solid woods and veneers
- Polished hardwoods to grain-painted pine
- Period re-creations
- Lacquering
- Woodcarving
- Water damage restoration

**1** Write down your own site theme or concept.
**2** Next, write down your initial thoughts on the theme-related topics you envisage having on your site.

## DESIGN YOUR WEB PAGES TO ATTRACT VISITORS

Whatever kind of site you intend building, a good website always aims to attract lots of visitors (referred to as traffic).

### PEOPLE SURF THE WEB FOR INFORMATION

In the physical world in which we live, people visit retail stores and shopping malls usually with the express intention of buying something they need or want. The World Wide Web is quite different: people surf the Web to find information. If the site they are visiting happens to offer some goods or services they're interested in, they may click on a link to make an online purchase, or to be contacted by the company in order to obtain more information. But, in all probability, they would not have come specifically looking for you in particular.

No one is going to visit your site unless you get two basic principles right:

- You need to provide good-quality, useful information that people are looking for; and
- People looking for that information need to find you – easily and quickly.

Certainly, people may find you by seeing your website address on your stationery, but (mostly) they find you by doing a search for what they're looking for – which is information. However, Web surfers are usually not prepared to wade through pages and pages of search results. Except for serious researchers, most people click on the websites listed on the first page or two of the search results, and if they don't find what they're looking for there, they will most likely start a new search with different search words. So, you need to be found easily by search engines, and you need your site to be listed on the first page or few of the search results. It is therefore essential that you construct your site in such a way that search engines will find you easily and list you in their top few pages, preferably their first page.

### How to get good traffic to your site

There are a few key tricks to getting traffic to your site, and these need to be attended to at the planning stage of website building, not only once your site has been completed. Here they are:

- Create a good number of Web pages, each containing high-quality, useful or interesting information related to your site concept and its topics – the kind of information that many people are looking for, usually with free access.
- Include in each Web page the words and phrases – known as keywords – that are most often entered into search engines by people who are looking for the information you are providing on that particular page.
- Make sure that there is not an over-supply of websites using those same search words or phrases; otherwise your site could end up far down the list of search results that the search engines display, and you'll never have many visitors to your site.

**FORMULA FOR HIGH TRAFFIC** A key strategy for attracting good traffic is to provide high-quality, in-demand content on a good number of pages, with each page containing high-demand keywords that don't have a huge over-supply of competing sites using those same keywords. Build your keywords and keyword phrases into several elements of your pages: the page title; page description; file names; link names; text content, and so on.

The first step in designing your site is therefore to find out which keywords you should incorporate into your Web pages. You need to do this *before* you start deciding the file names and detailed content of your pages. And it's better to do this with some research software than to take a wild guess at what you think people probably enter for their searches. Rather, get real statistics and do it properly. Also, doing keyword searches in this way usually brings up new keywords and keyword phrases one had not even thought of oneself. All-in-all, doing keyword searches is a very worthwhile exercise.

## KEYWORDS

Keywords are words or phrases that are entered into a search engine such as Google, Yahoo! and MSN by someone wanting to find some information on the Internet about a particular topic. For example, when searching for information on carrots, one might enter any of the following into the search engine window: *carrots, growing carrots, cooking carrots, organic carrots, carrot juice* or *how to grow big carrots.* Each one of these entries is regarded as a *keyword* even if it is a search entry consisting of several words.

## TIP: AVOID 'ANALYSIS PARALYSIS'

The processes that follow – for finding the level of demand and supply for your possible keywords – are important for increasing the likelihood of your website's being well positioned to attract visitors. It does take some time, but if you do it well, you will see benefit from the results. However, don't get bogged down in too much 'analysis paralysis' and frustration. Do what is *appropriate for your particular website and the target audience you're aiming at.* Know when to say 'Enough is enough!' for *your* particular situation. If you are planning to build a site for private viewing or by invitation only (e.g. a family or club site), then skip this next section and move on to the topic WRITE UP YOUR DETAILED CONTENT PLAN FOR EACH PAGE on page 23.

## FIND KEYWORDS THAT ARE IN HIGH DEMAND

The first step in this keyword analysis is to find the most frequently-searched keywords associated with your main theme, and also with each topic (page) of your site. To explain the process, we'll use our example of a website to be developed around the concept of wood furniture restoration and repair.

**DO A KEYWORD SEARCH FOR EACH TOPIC-RELATED PAGE** It is important that you do one of these searches for your home page (overall site theme) as well as for each topic or content page. The reason is that you need to optimize every page on your site for the search engines by having good keywords throughout your site. Because you'll be having different topics on each page, it stands to reason that you'll need keywords that relate to the topic of each individual page – because it is the *information* people are searching for, not your website. The information will be different on each page, and Web surfers will be entering search keywords related to the particular *topic* they're looking for.

## Install and open the Good Keywords software

1  Install the **Good Keywords** software that would have been extracted automatically to the **Programs** folder in My Webs. (If you need help with installing a program, go to our website's **Downloads** page and click on the link **Downloading and installing guidelines** and save the file to your computer for reference to the step-by-step procedures.)

2  Once installed, open **Good Keywords** on your screen.

## Search for keyword suggestions

1  Connect to the Internet.

2  In the Good Keywords main window, click on the **Keyword Suggestions** button to open the **Keyword Suggestions** window.

**3** Think of a likely **single word** that someone might enter into a search engine to find information about the **theme** of your website.

**4** Type this first (single) keyword into the **Base Keyword** text window, then click on the **Go!** button. (For the practice site – which is about the restoration of wood furniture – we used the word **furniture** as our first base keyword.)

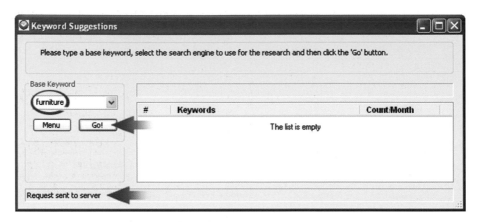

Search status shown in the lower grey panel of the window

Wait a few seconds while the program accesses data from the Internet search engines. After a short while the results of your 'lookup' will appear in the main window, ranked in terms of the number of searches in the preceding month that included the base keyword you entered.

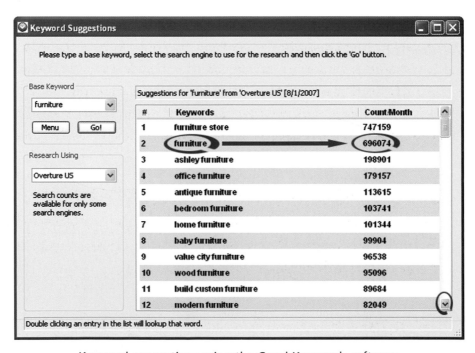

Keyword suggestions using the Good Keywords software

**5** Now, do another search using other keywords or phrases (e.g. the two words **wooden furniture** in our tutorial) and wait for the results (screenshot below left).

**6** Repeat with the two words **wood furniture** and wait for those results to be displayed (screenshot below right), and note the how the results differ dramatically when there is just a slight change in the keywords used in a search.

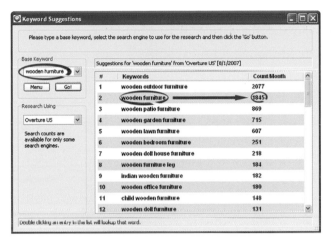

Search results for: *wooden furniture*

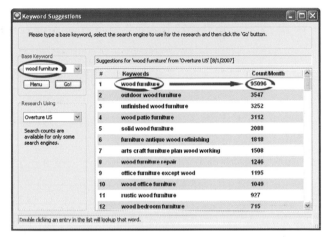

Search results for: *wood furniture*

**DO ADDITIONAL SEARCHES** The whole point of these searches is to find the best keywords, not merely to see how many searches were conducted last month on the keywords you have thought of. Taking the above examples – a search for *wooden furniture* and then a separate search using the words *wood furniture* – you'll see that just that slight difference in words yielded completely different results. So, it's important to do several searches with different base words and various phrases as well, in order to find additional suggested words or phrases that yield the highest number of monthly search entries. This exercise also demonstrates that the keywords we might assume to be the words most frequently searched, are not necessarily so. Often, completely different and surprising results come up.

**TIP: ALWAYS START WITH A BASE KEYWORD FIRST**

Do searches with a single ('base') keyword first, then search with keyword phrases emanating from the base keyword results – to make sure you don't miss any valuable high-demand keywords/phrases that should be incorporated into your content pages.

**TIP: LEARN MORE ABOUT THE GOOD KEYWORDS PROGRAM**

Before you do all your own searches for keyword suggestions, study the Help notes in Good Keywords (click on the Help button at the bottom of the main Good Keywords window) so that you know how to get the most out of this program.

## List the high-demand keywords appropriate for your site

Your next step is to extract from each of your several searches the keywords and phrases with high demand – those that you feel you'd be able to work into your site content quite easily.

1  Click on the Base Keyword ⌄ **down** arrow to access the list of searches you've done.

2  Click on the first search shown in the list.

3  Click on the **Go!** button to open the search results in the main window. (The results are retained until you right-click in the main window and click on **Remove This Result From History**.)

4  From the results list, select those items that have a high demand (say, over 10,000) and enter each one into a **Keyword Selection List** sheet (see Tip below).

5  Repeat steps 1 to 4 for each search you've done.

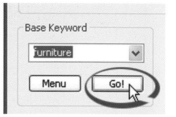

**TIP: DOWNLOAD OUR KEYWORD SELECTION LIST CALCULATOR**

If you have Microsoft Excel installed, you may want to download the Keyword Selection List Calculator file from our Website's **Downloads** page and enter your results into the Excel spreadsheet. It will calculate your Supply/Demand ratios for you automatically.

| Keyword Selection List | | | | |
|---|---|---|---|---|
| **Keyword/Phrases** | **Demand Stats** | **Supply Stats\*** | **Supply/ Demand Ratio** | **Best Keywords (✓)** |
| | (ex Good Keywords) | (ex Keyword Explorer) | (Demand ÷ Supply) x 100 | |
| furniture | 696,074 | | | |
| antique furniture | 113,615 | | | |
| home furniture | 101,344 | | | |
| wood furniture | 95,096 | | | |
| etc. | | | | |

\*Supply Stats is explained below.

## CHECK THE SUPPLY SITUATION FOR YOUR LISTED KEYWORDS

If you can isolate in your list of high-demand keywords/phrases those that have less competition (i.e. fewer sites offering pages that contain those same keywords), you can more confidently select a niche strategy for your site to attract a good number of visitors. Once your visitors are at your site, you can then offer them more than what they came for in the first place.

To do this supply analysis we'll use another program from Softnik Technologies, called Keyword Explorer. Besides just the raw statistics it generates, this program also gives you the URLs of the prominent Web pages that are ranking well for those keywords/phrases, so that you can visit them and see how those keywords have been used in the page content.

**1** Install and open the **Keyword Explorer** software (double-click on its **.exe** file in My Webs Programs); then connect to the Internet.

**2** From the Keyword Selection List you created, type the first keyword/phrase into Keyword Explorer's keyword window at the top.

**3** Under the **Market Region** heading (lower right of the window) click on the ⌄ **down** arrow to open the drop-down menu of regions (next screenshot on the right), and click on the region you wish to analyze. (We selected **US:United States** for our practice site.)

**4** Click on the **Analyze** button.

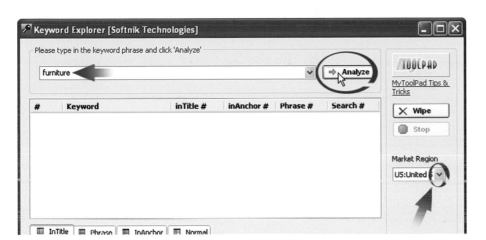

**5** Wait patiently for the word **Ready** to be displayed in the status bar at the bottom of the window, indicating that all the four lookups have now been completed (one lookup for each of the tabs above the list of URLs – *InTitle, Phrase, InAnchor, Normal*).

Waiting for more data

All data received

Once the lookup has been completed, the top pane will display the summary of the number of pages containing that keyword/phrase in the various page elements – page titles, anchors, phrases and the total number of pages. Details of the URLs where those keywords are used are given in the lower pane, under four different tabs: *InTitle, Phrase, InAnchor* and *Normal*.

Results of a supply search on furniture, as used in Web page titles

Once you've done a new search on each of the other keywords/phrases from your selection list, the window will display the summary data for those search results in the top pane, with the website details of the latest search shown in the lower pane. Be sure to wait until the search has been completed. This may take a while because a separate submission is sent to Google for each page element (title, phrase, etc.).

**6** To view the results of one of the other searches you've already done, simply click on that search in the top pane and its results will be displayed in the lower pane.

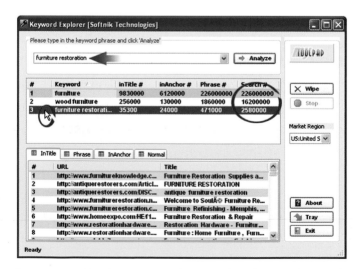

Lower pane in above screenshot: results of a supply search
on furniture restoration, as used in Web page titles

**NOTE: MORE HELP WITH KEYWORD EXPLORER**

For further details on Keyword Explorer's various functions, click on the **TOOLPAD** button in the Keyword Explorer window and explore their website.

## ANALYZE THE RESULTS

**1** Study the data, including the **page titles** used by your competitors (lower pane, Title column):
   ❏ Is there anything there you hadn't thought of for your initial list and demand searches?
   ❏ Are there any new keywords you haven't already done a demand search for in Good Keywords?

**2** Write down any new ideas and any additional keywords/phrases you want to do more research on (demand and supply searches).

**3** Enter the supply stats in the second column of your Keywords Selection List. (As a start, do this for the **inTitle#** column's stats first; then do it for the **Search#** column's stats as well, to get a good feel of what your searches are telling you.)

**4** Do more searches in **Good Keywords** and **Keyword Explorer** as necessary.

## Calculate the demand/supply ratios

Once you've entered both the demand and supply data into the respective columns of your Keyword Selection List, calculate the demand/supply ratio for each keyword and keyword phrase in your list (the Excel workbook will do this automatically as you enter the supply data).

**1** Divide the demand figure by the supply figure and multiply the answer by 100 – i.e. [Demand ÷ Supply] x 100; then write down the answer in the Ratio column – e.g. per our **wood furniture** example, in page titles, [Demand 95,096 ÷ Supply 256,000] x 100 gives a ratio of around 3.1).

## Decide which keywords are best for your site

Now it's time – if you haven't given up yet through analysis paralysis – to decide which keywords are likely to bring good traffic to your site – i.e. those words/phrases that are in high demand but which are not too heavily over-supplied. This will often include keywords and phrases that you had not initially thought of. That alone can make this process worthwhile for you.

Remember, over-supply means many, many websites/pages containing those keywords. This, in turn, means that it will be harder to get your site into the top listings. Wherever possible, you want to try to build into your site's content the keywords and phrases that have a high demand and a low supply, relative to other keywords in your list.

# DECIDE THE BROAD CONTENT PLAN FOR YOUR SITE

Using your keyword demand and supply ratios – for the words you originally thought of as well as any additional words or phrases that popped out through your searches – it's now time to make some decisions about your site content.

You need to determine whether the content you wish to provide in your various Web pages can in fact be written around those keywords – in page titles, page headings, page descriptions and page content text. If not, tweak your content as necessary so that it both meets your own needs while at the same time is likely to bring you good traffic.

If appropriate, consider adding new content topics that you hadn't thought of initially, but that you could indeed create around new keywords you've discovered – as long as those new topics somehow relate to your overall site concept.

Once you're satisfied that you can create good content material for each page – and that you can build into each page those keywords with a high search demand but without an over-supply of websites containing those same keywords – you should document this as your overall keyword-focussed site content plan (see example below). You'll then be ready to start designing the detailed architecture of your site.

## Overall keyword-related broad content plan

| Page topics | Keywords to be included in each page |
|---|---|
| **Website theme:**<br>Wood furniture restoration, refinishing and re-creation | wood furniture repair, wood furniture restoration, antique furniture restoration, furniture re-creation, stain finishes, faux finishes, paint refinishes, veneer repair, lacquering, water damage restoration, pick-up and delivery |
| **Topics** (in initial description terminology*): | |
| Testimonials from clients | teak, coffee table, furniture refurbished |
| Water damage restoration | water-damaged furniture, wood furniture |
| Services offered | stain finishes, faux finishes, lacquering, woodcarving, veneering, paint finishes, hand-crafted wooden, furniture restorations |
| Free useful tips (to build credibility) | wood care, furniture care, caring for wood furniture, waxing furniture, applying wax, antique wood furniture, natural woods |
| etc. | |

\* These would be as the thoughts come to you, and not necessarily the final page titles or page headings.

---

### TIP: EXPLORING KEYWORDS FURTHER

If you wish to explore the processes of search engine optimization (SEO) further – for your own website – here are a few websites you could visit. Be warned though: it can become somewhat confusing for an absolute beginner. So, approach the subject slowly, with caution, and try not to get bogged down by it all.

http://adwords.google.com — Explore their site to learn more.

http://www.globalpromoter.com — Remember to click on their **Free Tools** link too.

http://www.google.com — Do searches for **SEO** and for **search engine optimization** and explore the sites and pages that look useful.

# WRITE UP YOUR DETAILED CONTENT PLAN FOR EACH PAGE

It's now time to put pen to paper on the detailed content and architecture of your website. This means setting out on paper (or, better still, on your computer) the keyword-focussed detailed content of each page. This will be your website blueprint and should include the following:

- the page title (that appears in the blue Title bar in the visitor's browser)
- the page heading
- the page description
- what image/s are to be included on that page
- the links the page will have to other pages
- the text content (or 'copy'), and so on

At this first stage you'll not be too concerned about the page layout and design itself; the focus for now is on the content. The design and 'look-and-feel' of the site and its pages will be covered in a later chapter where you'll design the page template to be used for all your Web pages.

In this part of the planning process you'll type up the content you plan to have on each page, including the text 'copy', exactly how you intend to have it worded on that particular Web page.

### NOTE: READ THROUGH THIS NOW, BUT WORK WITH IT LATER

Once you've completed the step-by-step procedures for building the practice website with us (in the next three chapters), the following points will be useful to you when you come back and start working on your own site. For now, however, just read through the next two topics so that you have an understanding of what needs to be done before the individual Web pages are created.

## Some writing tips

In order for your website to attract visitors, as you develop your website blueprint you'll need to keep your focus continuously on several key elements, with an eye on consistency throughout your site.

- **Be brief:** Keep text crisp and succinct so your visitors can see immediately what your site is all about, and what it has to offer them. Remember most people are in a hurry to find what they're looking for.
- **Build credibility:** If it's a commercial site, your visitors don't know you or your reputation; they came there for information, not to buy. So, your content needs to build credibility and trust before they'll consider buying something from you.
- **Use clear language:** Write your sentences in plain, understandable language so that everyone understands what you're trying to convey. Avoid trying to impress with fancy terms and vocabulary.
- **Use headings:** Use headings and sub-headings to divide the paragraphs; use single lines for emphasis and make the paragraphs short – no more than four or five sentences per paragraph.
- **Use bulleted lists:** Lists and bullet points are a useful way of setting information out so that the eye can catch the key bits of information quickly.
- **Make text links meaningful:** Write the text for links to other pages in a way that it is clear as to what the visitor will find when they get to the linked page.
- **Be accurate:** Check your spelling and grammar carefully to avoid errors.

## Checklist for the content of each keyword-focussed page

You can use the following list to check each page's content specs as you go. (A copy of the checklist is available for download at our website so that you can make a copy for each page you'll prepare.)

❑ Is the page heading descriptive of what you want to get ranked well for?

❑ Is the page heading 15 words or less? (7 to 8 words is optimum for Google.)

❑ Does the page heading contain your best keywords relative to that page? (The closer together the keywords or key phrases are, the better – very important.)

❑ Is your page heading made up of text only (important for search engines), and not an image?

❑ Is the page content of a high calibre – spelling, grammar, accurate information, truthful? Will it be useful to your visitors?

❑ How many pages of interesting, quality content do you have? Google gives higher rankings to sites that have lots of quality information. If you have plenty of high-quality content pages you'll increase the likelihood that other sites will want to link to your site. Google will see you're getting more 'votes' and will increase your ranking accordingly.

❑ Does each page have its own unique page title, or heading, and does the title contain good keywords and content?

❑ Do the image file names include keywords too? When you start saving your images you will save each one incorporating the relevant keyword/s into the image's file name. For example, for our practice website on wood furniture restoration, we might name an image on a page as *RepairedCouchArm.jpg*, to incorporate that keyword into the image's file name, rather than have a file name like *image02.jpg*.

❑ Does each image also have a keyword in its text description (known as an *Alt tag*) – so that if users have their image display turned off they will see a description of the image instead? You should create a keyword-focussed image description for each of your images.

The following chart depicts an example of what a website's content blueprint might look like. We've underlined the keywords we've selected from the Keyword Selection List and Broad Content Plan to show how those keywords and phrases are being worked into each page's text.

# My Woodworking Website's Content Blueprint

(pages in random sequence at this stage – keywords underlined)

| Page properties | Details: keyword-related text and file names/tags for each page |
|---|---|
| **HOME PAGE** | **Site portal with overview and key links to site pages** |
| **Page file name:** | index.htm |
| **Page title:** | Woodsmithing Wood Furniture Restoration |
| **Page heading:** | Wood Furniture Restoration, Refinishing and Re-creation; North Vancouver, British Columbia |
| **Page description:** | Woodsmithing, Darren Smith - antique and contemporary wood furniture repair, restoration and re-creation. North Vancouver, BC, Canada. Free estimates and consultations. Insurance claims honoured. Excellent references available upon request. |
| **Images:**<br>• **tag descriptions**<br>• **file names** | • my company banner/logo<br>  ○ Tag: Woodsmithing Wood Furniture Restoration<br>  ○ File name: WoodsmithingBanner.jpg<br>• my photo, to show the face behind the business – up-front on the home page<br>  ○ Tag: Darren Smith – Woodsmith<br>  ○ File name: DarrenSmithPhoto.jpg |
| **Page content text:**<br>(If preferred, the content text can instead be typed in a separate text document containing only the text content of each page – in which case the next column would simply contain a reference to that document and page number.) | Woodsmithing is dedicated to the restoration, refinishing and re-creation of wood furniture including antique and contemporary treasures, from small, individual pieces (like storage boxes, games tables or individual chairs) to entire bedroom or dining-room suites. All work is to high standards of craftsmanship using the most durable materials available including fittings, fasteners, adhesives, paints, stains and waxes). Our projects range from solid woods to exquisite veneers and from finely polished hardwoods to grain-painted pine.<br><br>Darren Smith has spent his entire life surrounded by antiques, artefacts and art and grew up appreciating and being inspired by the natural beauty of wood and by the design and construction techniques employed by successive generations of North American and European furniture-makers. Darren is a graduate of a highly regarded cabinet-making program at Georgian College of Applied Arts and Technology.<br><br>*'I marvel at the natural beauty of wood and its strength and endurance as a building material. Every piece of furniture I see is an original piece of art because one of the most endearing qualities of wood is that no two pieces of wood are ever the same. The grain, the colour and the patterns within wood vary from tree to tree.'*<br><br>                                                   Darren Luther Smith |
| **Links:** | A navigation bar with links to all the tier one pages (see page 20 for diagram showing tiers).<br><br>To be filled in after completing a blueprint, and also a storyboard per the next topic. |

| | |
|---|---|
| **NEW PAGE** | **Actual case histories (before and after) of completed repair work** |
| **Page file name:** | casehistories.htm |
| **Page title:** | Woodsmithing Wood Furniture Restoration – Case Histories |
| **Page heading:** | Case Histories |
| **Images:**<br>• **tag descriptions**<br>• **file names** | • my company banner/logo<br>  ○ Tag: Woodsmithing Wood Furniture Restoration<br>  ○ File name: WoodsmithingBanner.jpg<br>• damaged antique sofa arm<br>  ○ Tag: Damaged Wood Arm of Antique Sofa<br>  ○ File name: ChewedCouchArm.jpg<br>• repaired sofa photo links to larger detailed photo<br>  ○ Tag: Repaired Wood Arm of Antique Sofa<br>  ○ File name: RepairedCouchArm.jpg as a link to: CouchArmLarge.jpg |
| **Page content text:**<br>(Can instead be typed in a separate text document containing the text content of each page.) | An example of some of the damage resulting from a puppy chewing and gnawing on both wood arms of this antique sofa.<br><br>Repaired arm of antique sofa. Click on the photo above to see close-up of repaired arm. |
| **Links:** | RepairedCouchArm.jpg links to large photo CouchArmLarge.jpg in new window<br>Standard navigation links to all tier-one pages |

# CREATE A STORYBOARD OF YOUR WEBSITE'S ARCHITECTURE

At this stage you will not have decided on the sequence of the pages or the links to other pages. To do this, it is useful to convert the key elements of your blueprint into what is called a storyboard – a rough, hand-sketched visual representation of the hierarchy of all your website pages. For example:

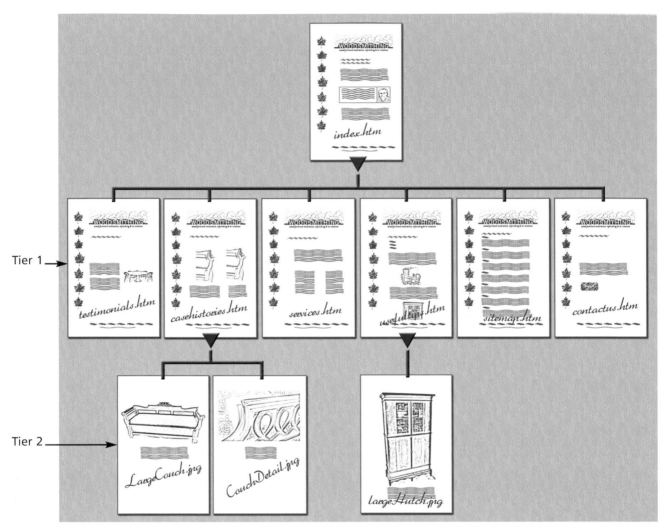

A typical storyboard for planning a website's architecture

A website storyboard will you save you time (and money) in the long run by providing a visual flow of information and architecture of your website before the development phase. Start by drawing a simple flow chart, then add all the elements (where you'll place the text, graphics and hyperlinks) to each page. A good, clean, clear navigation of a website is of vital importance, and a good storyboard will help you achieve this.

Once you've decided how your Web pages will 'hang together' and relate to one another, go back to your website blueprint document and enter the links that must be included on each page.

## ACTION SUMMARY FOR THIS CHAPTER

(once you're ready to develop your own site plan)

❏ Determine your site concept and goals.

❏ Use the Good Keywords program to get keyword suggestions for high demand keywords and phrases that are relevant to your site concept.

❏ Use Keyword Explorer to get the supply data for those keywords.

❏ Do additional searches as necessary.

❏ Calculate the Demand/Supply ratios and select the best keywords for your site.

❏ Set out your broad keyword-related content plan.

❏ Type the actual content text for each topic.

❏ Develop your website's content blueprint (see earlier example).

❏ Create a storyboard of your pages and organize the pages and links until you're happy with all aspects of the site, and that the links will work in a user-friendly way so that your visitors won't get lost or confused as they move from one link to another. This includes:

- how the various 'tier-one' content pages can be accessed from the home page navigation links;
- which 'tier-two' pages will be accessed from links on 'tier-one' pages;
- there is a good balance of text and images so that each page will load quickly;
- there are enough high-quality information pages to attract good search traffic.

❏ Go back to your website blueprint and amend it as necessary, because that will be the document you'll work from when you construct each Web page.

## THE NEXT STEP

In the next chapter you'll start organizing the images (photos, banners, buttons, etc.) that will be inserted into the various Web pages. In the process, you'll also be cropping, resizing and optimizing your images for use on a website. These preparatory steps are essential for saving time in page preparation and the eventual loading of the page in a browser, and also for ensuring that the images on your pages are actually displayed in the Web browser and not shown simply as a blank frame because the file path is incorrect.

# 3 Organizing your images

 **BUILD THE PRACTICE SITE WITH US** We recommend that you work through the hands-on, step-by-step procedures in the next few chapters to build a practice website with us. This will give you all the practical, hand-on experience you'll need for creating your own site later, by following the same procedures.

## GATHER ALL THE IMAGES YOU'LL NEED FOR YOUR SITE

Before you start creating your Web pages it is a good idea to locate all the images you'll be using for your website and save them into a special website folder that you should create somewhere in My Documents for this purpose. You could name it something like *Images for Websites*. These images could be digital photographs, your logo or crest, perhaps a banner to go across the top of each page, button graphics to be used as links to other pages, and any other images that are important for your particular site.

Depending on how your images are organized on your computer, this might take a while as you search for the ones you want for your website and save them to your *Images for Websites* folder. If you're unable to create your own graphics, do a search on the Internet and use such keywords as *website backgrounds, website buttons, free photos, free images,* and *free clipart*; you'll find a ton of resources you can choose from. Please respect copyright notices and never take what is not offered as a free download. Remember to save such items to your *Images for Websites* folder.

Many of the images you gather may not be ideally sized for use on a website, so you'll probably need to do some image resizing before you insert them into your Web pages. But for now, simply collect them and store them all together into the one *Images for Websites* folder.

### NOTE: EDITED IMAGES ARE SAVED LATER TO A DIFFERENT FOLDER

Note that the *Images for Websites* folder is not where you will eventually save your final, edited images (as explained in the next topic). It's more like an interim gathering point for your images from which you will make your final selection and do the image editing for your Web pages.

## EDIT THE IMAGES YOU'LL USE IN YOUR WEB PAGES

If you already have software that you can use to edit your images, then you'll probably know how to do that. If not, for now we suggest that you follow these steps to use the free photo editing program called Irfanview that is included in the files you would have downloaded via our website, and follow the procedures to edit the sample photo we've provided.

**IMAGE OPTIMIZATION FOR WEBSITES**

Large images on a Web page increase the time it takes for the page to load and be viewed. It is therefore important that images are edited for quickest loading time. Optimum viewing clarity is another factor to take into account, as is having your images cropped to exclude extraneous content that you don't want included in your final images.

Changing an image's physical size is called *image resizing*. Changing the resolution of an image by adding (or subtracting) pixels is called *resampling*. The physical size of the image (in centimeters/inches or in pixels) and its resolution, depicted in ppi (pixels per inch) determines the size of the file. 72 pixels per inch (ppi) is ideal for monitor viewing.

As for physical size, choose the smallest size you need, but one that will convey the effect and detail you wish your viewers to see. A size of 288 pixels x 288 pixels at 72 ppi will produce an image about 10 cm x 10 cm (4 inches x 4 inches), so any variation up to around that size would work well on a website. Bear in mind too that the eyesight of some viewers may not be as good as that of others. So you'll need to use your judgement when it comes to image size. Most basic image editing software can be used to resize an image and change its resolution. For simple line drawings, shapes or icons, it's best to use images in GIF format. For backgrounds and photographs, images in JPG (JPEG) format work best. Never use the bitmap file format for anything on a website.

## Install and open Irfanview

1  Use My Computer or Windows Explorer to browse to where you saved the Irfanview **.exe** file named **iview400.exe** (or a later version that you may have).
2  Double-click on the file to start the installation process
3  Follow the installation prompts provided by the program's supplier. (We recommend accepting the default offerings in the various dialog boxes that open.)
4  Once installed, open **Irfanview** on your screen. (If you prefer to have a white background rather than the default black, then click on **Options > Properties**, and in the **Properties** dialog box that opens, click the **Viewing** tab and change the **Main window color:** to white.)

## Crop out any extraneous content on your images

**1** Click on **File > Open** (or click on the Toolbar's ☞ **Open** icon – previous screenshot).

**2** Browse to My Documents\My Webs and double-click on the folder named **CropImage**, then click on the file named **DarrenDana.jpg** to select it.

**3** If not already checked, click on the check-boxes **Preview Active** and **Details** to see a thumbnail of the image and its key specifications.

**4** Click on **Open** to open the photo in Irfanview.

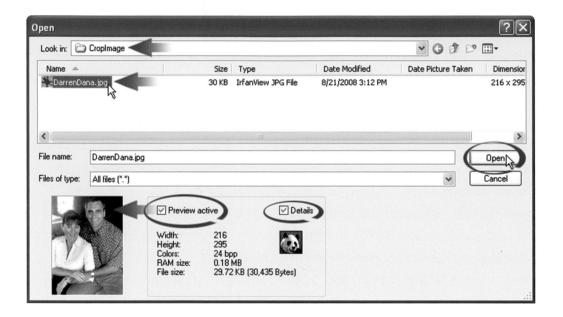

**5** Click at the top left corner of the area you wish to retain in the photo, hold the mouse button down, and drag the pointer to the bottom right corner of the required photo area, then release the mouse button. (The thin white frame – screenshot above right – will indicate the area that will be retained once you've cropped the photo.)

**6** To adjust that frame, click on the appropriate border and drag it out or in as necessary.

**7** To move the frame to a better position, right-click within the frame and drag.

**8** Once you're happy with the framed content, on the Menu bar, click on **Edit > Crop selection**, and the cropped image will now be displayed in Irfanview. (If it's not how you wanted it, click on **File > Reopen** to reload the uncropped image and start again; or simply click on the Toolbar ↺ **Undo** icon.)

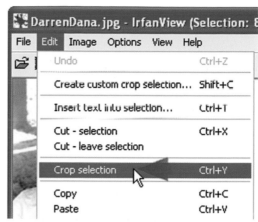

## Adjust the size and resolution of your images as necessary

1  With the cropped image still displayed in Irfanview, on the Menu bar click on **Image > Resize/Resample...** to adjust the image properties in the dialog box that opens.

2  In the lower left panel, make sure that the following option is ticked: **Preserve aspect ratio**; also select **Apply sharpen after Resample** if you want your image sharper.

3  In the little white box below that, type the resolution as **72** so that your Web page loading is not slowed down unnecessarily by a resolution much higher than is necessary for monitor viewing.

4  In the second panel on that side of the dialog box (higher up), click on the radio button **Set new size:** and select the **Units:** option you prefer (pixels, cm, or inches).

5  Type the required width into the **Width:** box, and the height measurement will adjust accordingly (because the aspect ratio has been preserved, per step 2 above).

6  When done, click on **OK**.

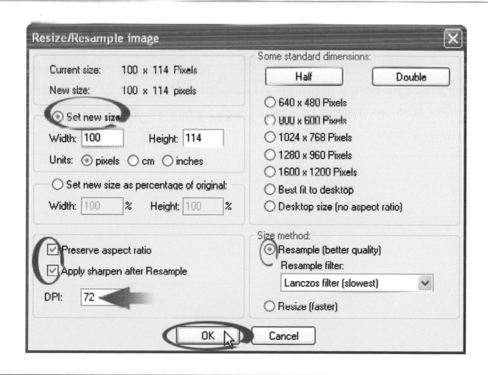

**7** Click on the Toolbar's 🖫 **Save as** icon to save the cropped and edited version into the **images** folder in My Webs\Woodsmithing.

**8** In the **Save Picture As...** dialog box that opens, change file name from DarrenDana to **DarrenAlone**, and in the **Save as type:** box choose **JPG – JPEG Files**, if it's not already selected.

**9** In the **JPEG/GIF save options** dialog box that opens alongside, de-select everything.

**10** Above that, set the quality to **80,** if it's not already set at 80. (This is called *optimizing* an image – a practical solution for reducing the sizes of images on Web pages.)

**11** Click on **Save**.

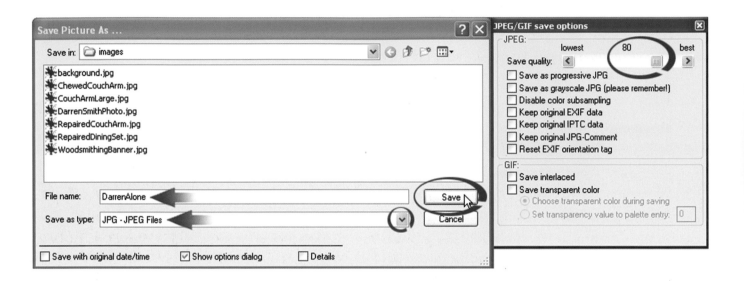

 **SAVE YOUR EDITED IMAGES TO THE CORRECT FOLDER** Once you've edited (resized, cropped, etc.) the images you will definitely be placing on your own Web pages, these should be saved in a special folder named *images*. Note that this particular folder's name is spelled all in lower case (no capital 'i') and it is stored within the folder of your particular website. The reason for this is that the folder's name and location will be included as part of the URL for that particular image, so the *images* folder name should be in lower case and within that particular website's folder on your hard drive. (For our practice site we've already edited all the images and saved them to the *images* folder inside *Woodsmithing*.)

## THE NEXT STEP

In the next chapter we'll (at long last!) start creating the Web pages themselves.

# 4 Creating a template

To avoid having to re-create every new page from scratch, and attempting to get each one's 'look and feel' to be exactly as the one before, it's much quicker and easier to set up a template in advance. The template would include, for example:

- the basic page layout as per your storyboard plan
- a banner across the top showing your website logo or corporate identity
- the background appearance if you want it other than plain white
- a navigation bar or column, showing the links to the other first-level pages on your site
- font styles and colours to be used throughout the site
- copyright information

Once you have your template designed and saved, it will be a breeze to complete each Web page by simply adding in the text content and graphics for that particular page.

---

### WEB PAGE AUTHORING SOFTWARE

Some word-processing programs, like Microsoft Word, can be used for designing Web pages, but they usually bring with them some inconveniences because they're not really designed for Web page creation. Most Web page authors prefer to use one of many dedicated programs developed specifically for designing Web pages, such as Microsoft Expression Web or Macromedia Dreamweaver, which come at a price most absolute beginners might prefer not to pay – unless they intend from the start to become professional website developers. Beginners often want to start with software that is somewhat less expensive, or even free. For this book you'll be using a neat and easy freeware application we've found on the Internet, called PageBreeze. It can be downloaded free of charge from a link on our own website at **http://www.ReallyEasyComputerBooks.com**.

---

## INSTALL AND OPEN THE PAGEBREEZE SOFTWARE

1 Browse to where you saved PageBreeze, and double-click on the file named **pgbreeze.exe** (or a later version with a different file name, if that's what you have) to start the installation process.
2 Follow the installation prompts provided by the program's supplier. (We recommend accepting the default offerings in the various dialog boxes that open.)
3 Once installed, if necessary double-click on the Desktop shortcut icon to open **PageBreeze** on your screen.

Note the tabs across the top of the welcome page; PageBreeze opens at the Normal (editing) tab.

## START A NEW TEMPLATE FILE

1   On the left of the PageBreeze Toolbar, click on the ⬜ **New Page** icon to open the **Create New Page** dialog box.

2   In the **Page Title** text window (see next screenshot), type: **WoodsmithingTemplate**

3   Under the heading **Base this new page on a template**, click on **_blank_arial_style.htm** to select it (because we're now going to create our own customized template from scratch with the font style already pre-determined).

4   Under the **File Location** heading in the dialog box, double-click on **C:\** then browse to **My Webs\Woodsmithing** (which should be located at C:\My Documents, although yours could be a different hierarchy, depending on how your computer has been set up – see the next blue tip box).

5   Double-click on the **Woodsmithing** folder to open it.

6   Click on **OK** to close the box and display the beginnings of your new template.

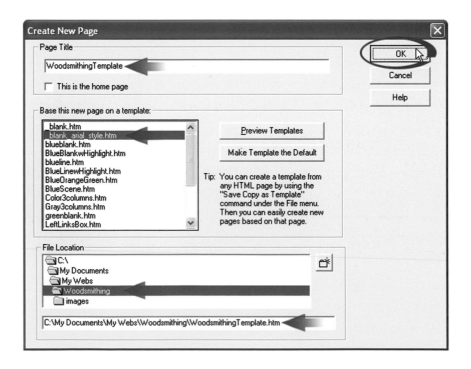

**TIP: FINDING THE WOODSMITHING FOLDER IN 'MY WEBS'**

Depending on your setup, in PageBreeze you may need to double-click on **C:\**, then on **Documents and Settings**, then on **Administrator** (or **All Users**), then on **My Documents**, and scroll down to find **My Webs** and double click on it to display the **Woodsmithing** folder.

The file **WoodsmithingTemplate.htm** (with Arial as the default font style) is now automatically saved into the **Woodsmithing** folder in **My Webs** – see lower left pane in the following screenshot – and the page title is displayed in the Title bar at the top of PageBreeze. (You'd obviously use your own suitable file name when you build your own site.) The elements common to all the pages on this site will be added in the topics that follow.

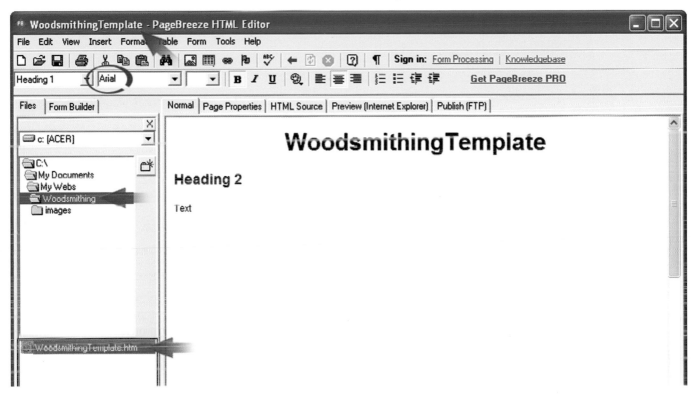

The beginnings of a new Web page template being created in PageBreeze

**NOTE: PAGEBREEZE'S BUILT-IN TEMPLATES**

PageBreeze's own built-in templates can be explored later. (They're stored under **C:\Progam Files\PageBreeze\Templates**.) For now, you're going to learn how to create your own template from scratch, which will enable you to customize your pages completely to your own requirements – and it's much more creative and fun too.

**7** Click on the **Page Properties** tab.

**8** In the **Title** window, delete the text WoodsmithingTemplate and type:
**Woodsmithing Wood Furniture Restoration**

**9** Leave the Meta Tags window (below that) blank at this stage because each page will have its own tags that will be relevant to that particular page (see blue text box below).

**10** Click on the Toolbar 🖫 **Save** icon to save the changes.

**11** When done, click on the **Normal** tab to revert to the editing mode.

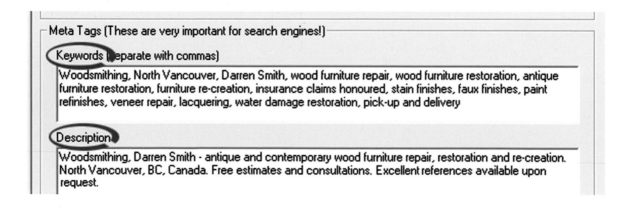

| Normal | Page Properties | HTML Source | Preview (Internet Explorer) | Publish (FTP) |

Page Attributes

Title  Woodsmithing Wood Furniture Restoration

Set Page Background...

Style Sheet    Edit...

Meta Tags (These are very important for search engines!)

Keywords (separate with commas)

---

### NOTE: ADDING META TAGS SEPARATELY TO EACH PAGE

As explained in Chapter 2, each page covers its own topic and requires its own content-related keywords. Likewise, it will have its own content-related page title and page description. These details are entered separately for each page, using the **Page Properties** tab as shown above. The screenshot below shows how this information would be entered into the text windows for the home page (**index.htm**). This will be done in Chapter 5 when you create each individual Web page. Each other page will in turn have its own details too.

---

Meta Tags (These are very important for search engines!)

Keywords (separate with commas)

Woodsmithing, North Vancouver, Darren Smith, wood furniture repair, wood furniture restoration, antique furniture restoration, furniture re-creation, insurance claims honoured, stain finishes, faux finishes, paint refinishes, veneer repair, lacquering, water damage restoration, pick-up and delivery

Description

Woodsmithing, Darren Smith - antique and contemporary wood furniture repair, restoration and re-creation. North Vancouver, BC, Canada. Free estimates and consultations. Excellent references available upon request.

**TIP: SET PAGEBREEZE TO OPEN EACH TIME AT THE LAST PAGE YOU WORKED ON**

Whenever PageBreeze is loaded, by default it opens at C:\Program Files\PageBreeze. This means you need to browse in order to get back to where you were last working (in My Documents\My Webs and the website you were working on). You can save yourself some time by setting PageBreeze to open each time at the last page you had open on your screen, with the correct folder hierarchy displayed in the left-hand pane of the PageBreeze window. Click on **Tools** > **Settings...** and click in the first check-box to select it, then click on **OK**.

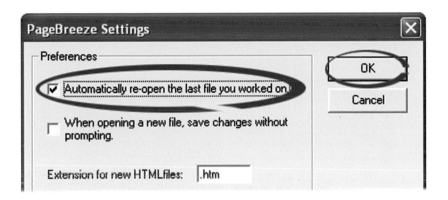

## INSERT THE PAGE BACKGROUND COLOUR

**1** With the template **WoodsmithingTemplate.htm** still open, hold down the `Ctrl` key and press `A` to select the entire contents of the page; then press the `Del` key to clear it all and be left with a blank page.

**2** Click on the **Page Properties** tab, then click on the **Set Page Background** button (screenshot below left).

**3** In the **Set Page Background Properties** dialog box that opens, click on the **Choose...** button opposite **Set Background Color:** to open the **Page Color** dialog box.

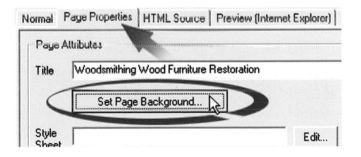 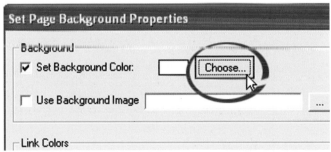

**4**   In the **Basic Colors:** palette on the left of the **Color** dialog box, click on the colour with the nearest match to the background colour you desire (in our case **yellow**); the pointer (three black selection marks) will move to the yellow colour in the color matrix on the right of the **Color** dialog box.

**5**   Click and drag the **pointer** (inside the colour matrix) horizontally to select colours (or hues) and vertically to select that colour's saturation.

**6**   Click and drag the black **slider** arrow on the right to adjust the luminosity (brightness or darkness) of the selected colour – see blue tip box below.

**7**   If you know the exact numerical values of the colour you require, type them into the boxes below the color matrix instead of dragging the pointer and slider.

**8**   When done, click on **OK**.

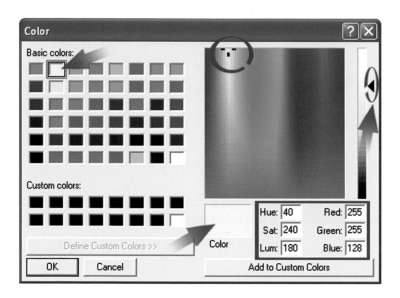

### TIP: KEEP A NOTE OF YOUR OWN NUMERICAL VALUES

When creating colours for various backgrounds on your own website, look at the colour sample in the little **Color** window to the left of the numerical values. Since all colours are comprised of red, green and blue (RGB), the Hue, Saturation and Luminosity values adjust accordingly when the numerical RGB values are entered. Once you're happy with your choice, make a note of the Red, Green and Blue numerical values for future use, so that you can accurately re-create that colour whenever you need to. You can also add that colour to the list of Custom Colors for your website by clicking on the button **Add to Custom Colors**. However, we recommend that you still keep a note of the values.

## Select the exact colour for the practice website

To change the primary yellow offered in **Basic colors** to the soft beige used for the practice site, do the following:

**1** Type the following colour values into the three boxes in the right-hand column below the color matrix: Red **248**, Green **248**, Blue **233**.

**2** Click on the **Add to Custom Colors** button to add that colour to the palette of Custom Colors for future quick access.

**3** Make a written note of those numerical values for future reference.

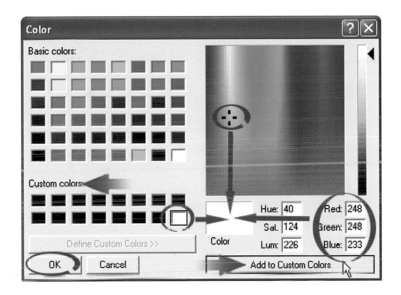

**4** Click on **OK** again to close the Set Page Background Properties dialog box.

**5** Click on the **Normal** tab to get back to the template page which will now display the new background colour.

**6** Click on the Toolbar's 🖫 **Save** icon to save the changes.

## Adding an image as a background

You can also add an image as the page background, in which case the background image will hide the background colour that was chosen from the colour palette/matrix, once the page has fully loaded and provided that the browser's images display option is not turned off.

> **TIP: USE A BACKGROUND COLOUR EVEN WHEN USING A BACKGROUND IMAGE**
>
> Even if you decide to use a background image, it's useful to have a background colour so that, in our example, the soft beige background is what shows when the rest of the site is still loading. Also, if the visitor to your site has the background images turned off in their browser, a background colour will still be visible because it's not an image file.

**1** Click on the **Page Properties** tab; in the **Set Page Background Properties** dialog box, click on the **Set Page Background** button, then on **Use Background Image**.

**2** Click on the ⬚ **browse** button (to the right of the Use Background Image window) to open the **Select Graphic** dialog box, and browse to and double-click on the **images** folder inside My Webs\Woodsmithing to open it.

**3** Click on the pre-prepared **background.jpg** file to select it; then click in the check-box beside **Preview Image** to view a sample of the image.

**4** Click on **OK** to close and return to the Set Page Background Properties dialog box.

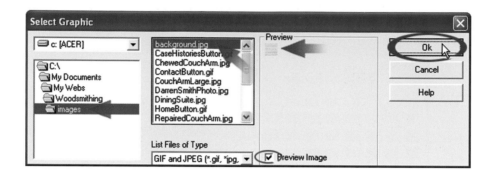

## Set the default font colour

**1** Still in the Set Page Background Properties dialog box, under Link Colors click on the **Choose** button opposite **Select Text Color:**.

**2** From the colour palette click on the **Brown** colour.

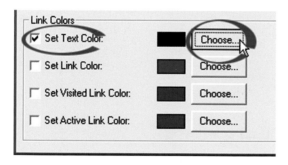
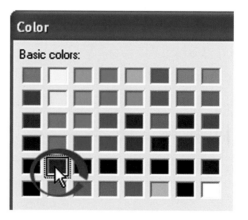

**3** Click on **OK** to close the Color dialog box and return to the Set Page Background Properties dialog box, and click on **OK** again to close that box too.

**4** Click on the **Normal** tab to see your new background addition (the font colour will obviously show only when text is added).

**SAVE YOUR CHANGES FREQUENTLY** To avoid losing your work that has taken valuable time to create, be sure to save the page again after each change you've made, and/or every few minutes.

## INSERT A TABLE TO FRAME YOUR CONTENT

You may have wondered how Webmasters manage to position their text and images exactly where they want them, with no visible indication of how the page setup allows for that. It's done by creating tables with no visible borders, and adding additional tables and cells within the main table. Tables also allow you to constrain the width of the page content so that your content doesn't fill the entire width of the browser's window – a sure sign of a novice page designer.

1 On the Menu bar, click on **Table > Insert Table...**.

2 In the **Insert Table** dialog box that opens, set the table properties. (For the practice site, set the properties to the specifications as shown in the screenshot below.)

3 In the **Background/Colors** panel, click in the check-box **Set Background Color**, then click on **Choose...** to open the **Color** palette, and choose the colour from the colour palette/matrix per the steps already explained for the page background colour. (In order to give the appearance of a dark border around the table, use the following numerical values for the colour background of the main table: Red **204**, Green **204**, Blue **153**.)

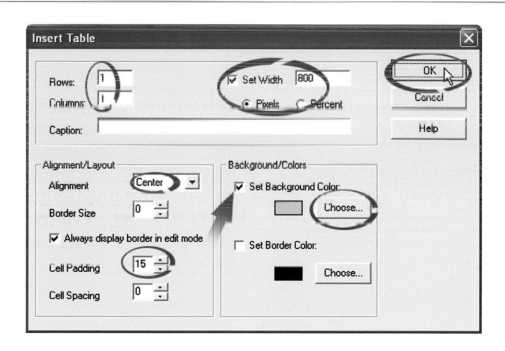

---

**CELL PADDING**

One use of cell padding is to prevent text and images inside a table from touching the edges of the table – in other words, to create an invisible margin within the table/cell. This is important when a table's background colour is different from the page's background colour.

In our practice site we're using the padding feature to create a coloured frame (not a *border*, which is something different) around our main table without using the **Border Size** option. Different browsers display borders in different ways, the results often not ending up as desired. So, padding the main table creates a coloured frame that displays consistently in all browsers. We've used 15 pixels for padding around our main table.

---

In Normal view, the top of your template page, with its first table, should now look like this:

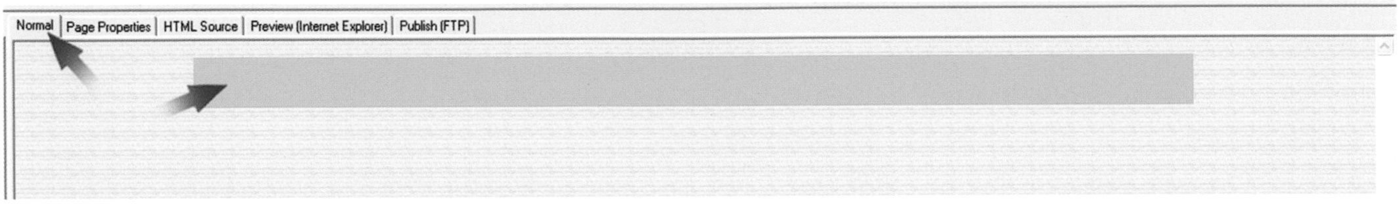

## INSERT NESTED TABLES WITHIN THE MAIN TABLE

**DEFINITIONS: TABLES, CELLS, NESTED TABLES**

A table with only one row and two columns consists of two *cells*: ☐☐ . If another two-cell row is added, the table – with two columns and two rows – now has four *cells*: ⊞ . A nested table is a table that has been inserted into another table's cell. A *nested table* can also have one cell, or several rows and columns (giving it several cells).

For our practice site we'll insert into the main table a nested table with two columns and two rows so that you can position the various components (navigation buttons, text areas, images, etc.) correctly on the page template. The page will then have a table structure as shown below, with the red and blue borders used here to indicate the two separate tables. To see the table's borders in Normal view, on the Menu bar click **View > Borders** if it isn't already selected.

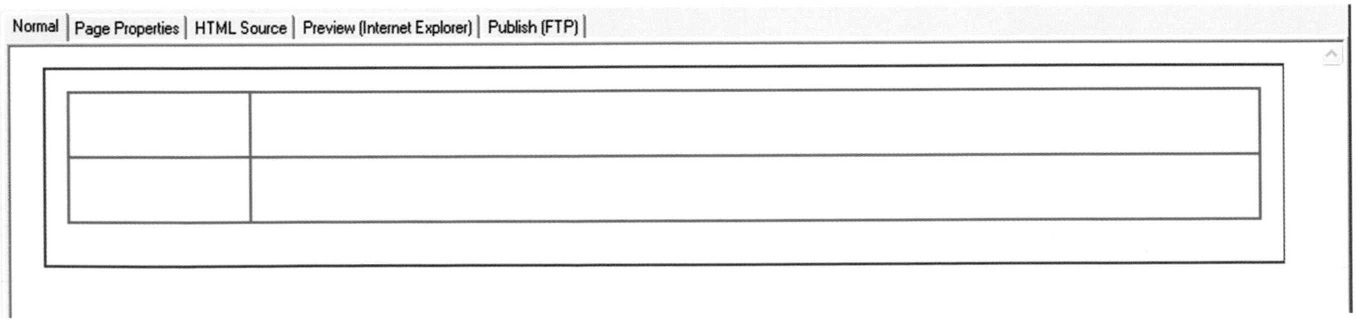

Red border indicates the main table
Blue border indicates the nested 4-cell table

**NOTE: TABLE STRUCTURE AND DIMENSIONS**

The width of the practice site's main table – shown with a red border in the previous diagram – will be 800 pixels, including its padding. The width of the nested table inside it – shown with a blue border in the diagram – will fill the main table 100% up to the padding. The nested table will have two rows and two columns. We made the first column 100 pixels wide, which is enough to accommodate the navigation buttons/links that will be positioned one beneath the other in the center of that top left-hand column (using *horizontal alignment:* **center**), and starting from the top of that column (using *vertical alignment:* **top**). We have not given a numerical value to the width of the *second* column of the nested table as it's only the left column that needed to be set with a pre-determined pixel width, but we have specified the *vertical alignment* of the second column also as: **top**. The nested table's second row of two columns will be used for the site's navigational text links that will be displayed at the bottom of the page, beneath the main content text that will be entered into the first row of the second column.

Here's a screenshot of what we're aiming at for the finished page template:

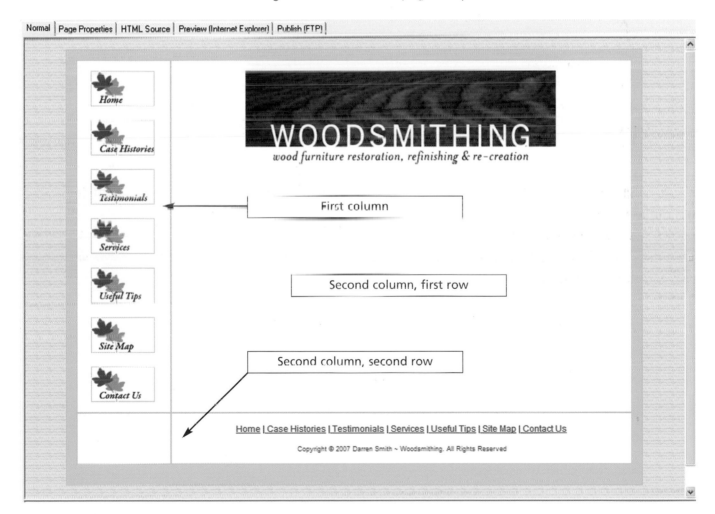

In Normal (edit) view, showing the table's structure

To achieve this structure for the practice site, you need to do the following:

1 Click inside the main table and, on the Menu bar, click on **Table > Insert Table...**.
2 Set the properties to the new specifications as shown in the screenshot below.
3 Under **Background/Colors**, click in the check-box **Set Background Color**, then click on **Choose...** to open the **Color** palette, and this time select the custom colour you added for the page background. (If you didn't save it as a custom colour, type these values into the right-hand column again: Red **248**, Green **248**, Blue **223**.)

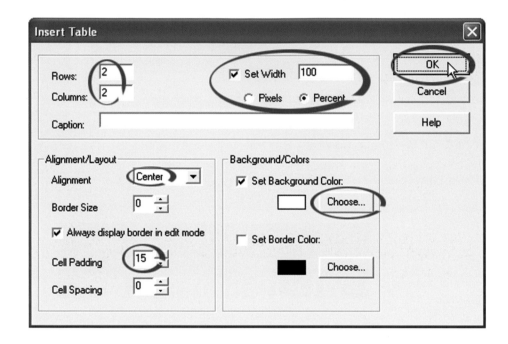

In Normal view, the nested table (with the lighter background) should look like this, before changing the column widths. Note the darker green padded area around the main table.

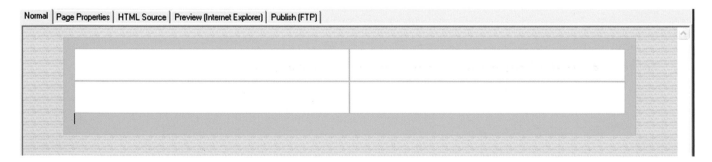

# SET THE COLUMN WIDTHS AND CONTENT ALIGNMENTS

## Set the first column of the nested table

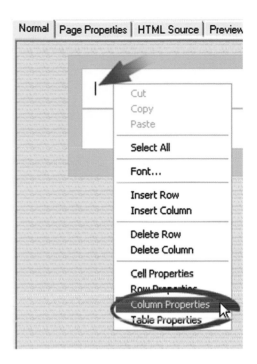

1 Right-click inside the top **left** cell (the first column and row) of the nested table to open a drop-down menu.
2 Click on **Column Properties** to open the **Column Properties** dialog box.
3 Set the table's properties to the specifications as shown in the screenshot below:
   **Horizontal Alignment: Center** – so that the buttons will be centred in the column.
   **Vertical Alignment: Top** – so that the buttons will start at the top of the column, and not lower down.
   **Set Width: 100 pixels** – just enough to accommodate the navigation buttons.
4 When done, click on **OK** to close the Column Properties dialog box.

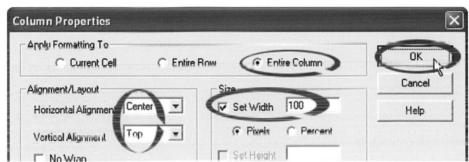

5 Next, right-click inside the top **right-hand cell** of the nested table.
6 Click on **Cell Properties** to open the **Cell Properties** dialog box
7 Set the **Vertical Alignment:** at **Top** (as per the screenshot below).
8 When done, click on **OK** to close the Column Properties dialog box.

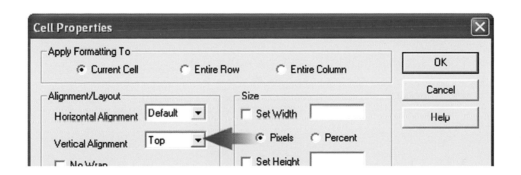

> ### TIP: SELECT THE CORRECT MEASUREMENT UNITS
>
> When setting the size (width or height), always make sure you select the appropriate units – pixels or percent – depending on what you're trying to achieve.

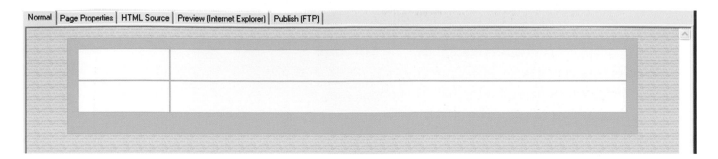

The completed table layout for the practice site

## ADD A BANNER TO THE TEMPLATE

A banner is a company logo or banner. You can either create your own in a graphics program or, as we have done for the practice site, simply scan the company's logo off its letterhead or business card and use the JPEG image file as the site banner.

### Inserting a banner in graphic format

1   On the Toolbar, click on the 🖼 **Insert Graphic** icon (or on the Menu bar click on **Insert > Insert Graphic…**).
2   In the **Insert Graphic** dialog box (see opposite), double-click on the **images** folder in My Documents\My Webs\Woodsmithing and click on the image file named **WoodsmithingBanner.jpg** to select it.
3   In the **Alternate Text** window, type: **Woodsmithing Wood Furniture Restoration**. (This is important for people who have graphics turned off in their Web browser; but, more importantly, the **Alt text** on images is recognized by search engines as page text.)
4   Note that the **Size** of the graphic is entered automatically by PageBreeze. (The size attributes act as a placeholder while the site is loading; and if images are turned off in the browser, they prevent the text from moving into the space reserved for the image.)
5   Click on **OK**, and the banner image will be inserted into the Web page.

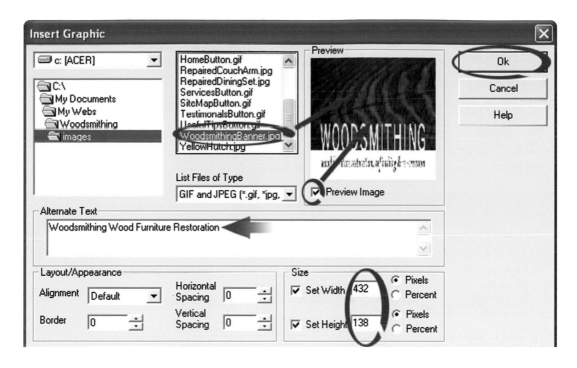

6  To centre the banner in the cell, click on the banner image to select it.

7  On the Formatting Toolbar, click on the ≡ **Center** icon; save the changes.

## Preview your page in Internet Explorer view

To follow your progress and see exactly what the page will look like in a browser window, as opposed to the edit view you're working in:

1  Click on the **Preview (Internet Explorer)** tab.

2  When you want to return to the editing window, click on the **Normal** tab on the left.

### NOTE: TABLE AND CELL BORDERS ARE DISPLAYED IN EDIT ('NORMAL') VIEW

By default, the borders of tables and cells are displayed in **Normal** (edit) view (see screenshot on page 46), but not in **Preview (Internet Explorer)** view. The default can be changed, if you wish, by clicking on **Table > Table Properties** and un-checking **Always display border in edit mode**. But, for editing purposes, it is useful to be able to see the table borders.

## INSERT THE NAVIGATION BUTTONS

This procedure is the same as the one for inserting a banner, because they are images you are inserting. You can either use a graphics program to create your own customized buttons – as we've done for our practice site – or you can find ready-made buttons, free for the taking, on the Internet. Another option, of course, would be to use text for the links, instead of buttons.

**1** To insert the first button, click in the **left cell** of the beige nested table.

**2** On the Toolbar, click on the 🖼 **Insert Graphic** icon.

**3** In the **Insert Graphic** dialog box, double-click on the **images** folder in My Documents\My Webs\Woodsmithing and click on the image file named **HomeButton.gif** to select it.

**4** In the window beneath **Alternative Text**, type **Woodsmithing Home Page**.

**5** Click on **OK** to close the dialog box.

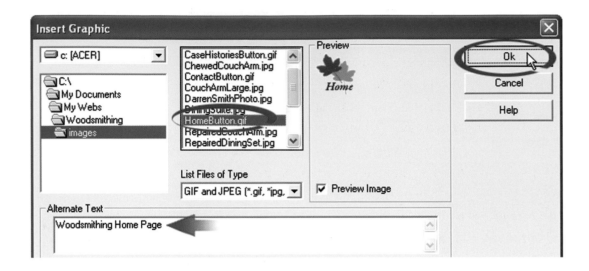

**6** Click to the right of the **Home** button and press the ⏎ Enter key to drop down one line before inserting the next button.

**7** Repeat steps 2 to 5 to insert the button **CaseHistoriesButton.gif**.

**8** Continue like this to add the remaining navigation buttons until all seven have been inserted into the template: **HomeButton.gif, CaseHistoriesButton.gif, TestimonialsButton.gif, ServicesButton.gif, UsefulTipsButton.gif, SiteMapButton.gif** and **ContactButton.gif** (see page 43 for a full-page screenshot).

### NOTE: THE HYPERLINKS WILL BE ADDED SEPARATELY

At this stage we're inserting the navigation buttons and the separate navigation texts. These will then be made into hyperlinks once this topic has been completed.

# INSERT THE NAVIGATION TEXT

When using icons or buttons for links to the other pages on your website, or to other external websites, it is imperative also to include text links to the same pages in order to accommodate different operating systems, different browsers, as well as visitors who have images turned off in their browsers. A simple horizontal row of text links located at the bottom of your webpage – each link separated by a vertical bar – is all that is necessary. We created the second row in our original nested table for this purpose. By placing the navigational links in this bottom row, they're sure to remain consistently at the bottom of each page, no matter how much or how little page content there is on each of your different Web pages.

**1** Click in the bottom right-hand cell to select it, and type the words that will later become additional hyperlinks to each of the tier-one pages on your website; and separate each piece of text by a space, a vertical line and another space. (To type a vertical line, hold down the [Shift] key and press the [|] keyboard key.) Type as follows:

Home | Case Histories | Testimonials | Services | Useful Tips | Site Map | Contact Us

**2** Click on the ≡ **Center** icon to centre the links in that cell.

**3** Press [Enter] once to drop down a line.

**4** Next, insert your **copyright** information below the text links. (For the practice site, type: **Copyright © 2007 Darren Smith ~ Woodsmithing. All rights reserved.**)

**5** Select and format the copyright text line to font size **1**, and centre the text in the cell.

## BONUS TIP: INSERTING SYMBOLS

Click on **Start** > **All Programs** > **Accessories** > **System Tools** > **Character Map**, and scroll through the window of symbols displayed in the Character Map dialog box. Click on the symbol you require, and an enlarged view of it will be displayed. Click on **Select** and the symbol will be displayed in the **Characters to copy:** box. Then click on **Copy**. Return to the Web page and click on **Paste** to paste the symbol into the page. You can change the font by clicking on the [v] down arrow at the top of that dialog box.

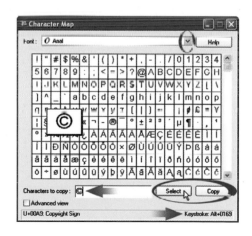

Where available, an optional keystroke shortcut is indicated at the bottom right corner of the Character Map dialog box. For the copyright symbol, you could simply hold down the **Alt** key and type **0169** on the **numbers keypad**. (This may, however, not work on a keyboard without a separate numbers keypad – e.g. some laptops.)

## CREATE THE HYPERLINKS

Now that the navigation buttons and texts are in place, it's time to convert them into hyperlinks which, when clicked on, will take the viewer to the linked page.

---

**TIP: REFER TO YOUR SITE BLUEPRINT**

When you create your site blueprint (Chapter 2), that is when you decide the file name for each Web page. Knowing your pages' file names before you create your template enables you to include on your template the hyperlinks to all the tier-one pages of your site even before you've actually created and saved those pages. In this way, your template will be as complete as possible in terms of the items that are common to all pages, and you'll save yourself a lot of time when creating the various pages of your website.

---

**1** Click on the first navigation button **Home** to select it.

**2** Click on the Toolbar's ☜ **Insert/Edit Hyperlink** icon to open the dialog box.

**3** In the External URL window near the bottom, delete the text **http://** and type the **file name** of the page to which that link will take you (refer to the list of link items and filenames with the next screenshot – e.g. **index** for the home page).

**4** Click on **OK**, and the button will become a hyperlink.

**5** Repeat steps 1 to 4 for each navigation button, typing that particular link's file name in the External URL window (e.g. services, usefultips, etc.).

**6** Next, select the first **text link** in the second row of the nested table (near the bottom of the page), and insert the appropriate link by following steps 1 to 4 above; save the changes.

**7** Repeat these steps to create a hyperlink for each of the other text links.

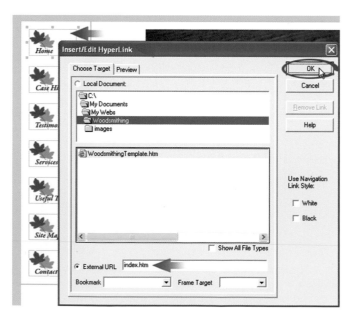

| Link item | Type this file name |
|---|---|
| Home | index |
| Case Histories | casehistories |
| Testimonials | testimonials |
| Services | services |
| Useful Tips | usefultips |
| Site Map | sitemap |
| Contact Us | contactus |

**NOTE: LOCAL DOCUMENT VERSUS EXTERNAL URL**

Because we are creating hyperlinks that will be common to all *tier-one* pages, we're inserting those links into the template before creating any of the Web pages themselves. Once you start building individual Web pages based on the template, on some of those pages you may have hyperlinks to some *tier-two pages* – that is, pages that are offshoots from a particular *tier-one* page but not linked directly from *all* of the tier-one pages. When these non-common links are created, in the Insert/Edit Hyperlink dialog box you would then select an existing Web page from the Local Document window, instead of typing into the External URL box the file name of a page that hasn't yet been created. This will be clarified further and demonstrated in the next chapter.

## THE NEXT STEP

Now that the time-consuming part of the template-building process has been completed, it's time to move on to the next chapter where you'll insert the unique content into each of the Web pages making up the website.

# 5 Building the pages

In this chapter we'll build the content into each page of the website, using the template as the basic design for each page. Specifically, this is where you will:

- save the template as each new page with its own file name;
- insert the page titles, headings and text content relevant to each individual page;
- format the headings and sentence text (font styles, sizes and colours);
- insert and position the images;
- insert any additional links specific to a particular page, which are not part of the template.

---

**TIP: CREATE A BACK-UP COPY OF YOUR TEMPLATE**

At this point, it's a good idea to save a backup copy of your website template. After working so hard on it, it would be frustrating and time-wasting to have to start all over because the template was lost due to a glitch or an error on your part. A good place to save a backup is in PageBreeze's Templates folder. With your template open, click on **File > Save Copy as Template**, and a **Save Copy as Template** dialog box will open. (You will see all of PageBreeze's template options listed.) Simply click the **Save** button and your own template will now be stored in a safe place in the event that you should ever need it. To retrieve your template, browse to C:\Program Files\PageBreeze\Templates.

---

## CREATE A SEPARATE .HTM FILE FOR EACH PAGE

1 In the top window of the PageBreeze **Files** pane on the left, double-click on the website's folder (**Woodsmithing** for the practice site) to open it and display the .htm files in the lower pane.

2 Double-click on the template file to open it – in the practice site it's the one named **WoodsmithingTemplate.htm**.

3 Click on **File > Save As...** (NB: not just Save, but **Save As...**).

4 In the **File name:** window of the **Save As** dialog box, type the name **index** to overwrite the highlighted **WoodsmithingTemplate.htm** name, and click on the **Save** button; the new file's name (**index.htm**) will be displayed in the lower pane of the left-hand **Files** window (see screenshot on the right).

**NOTE: THE HOME PAGE FILE NAME**

Most websites' home pages are normally given the file name index.htm – or index.html. This is true particularly if you have your own domain name and only want your domain name to show as the site address, e.g. http://www.reallyeasycomputerbooks.com. (PageBreeze is set by default to use the shorter **.htm** extension for all saved Web pages but you can change that to **.html** if you choose.)

**5** With the current page still open:
  - Click on **File > Save As...** again, and save the file as the next Web page's file name (for the practice site, call it **casehistories**).
  - In the **Page Properties** tab, add the words **Case Histories** at the end of the **Page Title** (i.e. **Woodsmithing Wood Furniture Restoration - Case Histories**)
  - Be sure to save the changes.

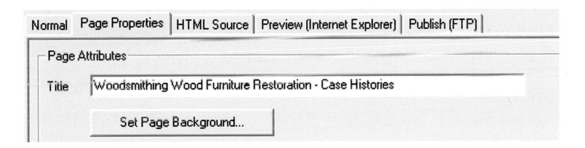

Note that when you reopen that page, the new page title will be displayed in the Title bar at the top of PageBreeze, which means the same page title will display in all browsers.

**6** Repeat step 5 for each Web page on the site, using the page titles and file names given below, until all the saved files are displayed in that lower **Files** pane – screenshot on the right; and remember to save after each page is created. (There's no need to reopen the template page each time; simply use the page that's currently open and save that one as the new page file.)

| Save as file name: | Change page title to: |
|---|---|
| index | Woodsmithing Wood Furniture Restoration |
| casehistories | Woodsmithing Wood Furniture Restoration - Case Histories |
| testimonials | Woodsmithing Wood Furniture Restoration - Testimonials |
| services | Woodsmithing Wood Furniture Restoration - Services |
| usefultips | Woodsmithing Wood Furniture Restoration - Useful Tips |
| sitemap | Woodsmithing Wood Furniture Restoration - Site Map |
| contactus | Woodsmithing Wood Furniture Restoration - Contact Us |

**TYPE ACCURATELY** Be sure to type every Web page's file name 100% accurately; otherwise, the links will not work because the browser won't be able to find the page you're linking to. Web page file names cannot have spaces between the words. If you need to separate words in file names, then use a hyphen ( - ) or an underscore ( _ ) to do this. But for the practice site type the file names exactly as we've shown them.

## OPEN THE DEMO WEBSITE IN YOUR BROWSER

### NOTE: THE DEMO SITE VERSUS THE PRACTICE SITE

To clarify again, there are **two** websites for Woodsmithing that you will be working with in these tutorials – a **practice** site, and a **demo** site. The **practice site** is the one for which the template was created in Chapter 4, and for which the individual pages are being constructed in this chapter. The **demo** site is a fully functional mini-version of the Woodsmithing website, which we have created especially for this book. You can open the demo site in your browser (see next step-by-step box) in order to see how it functions and what the individual pages look like. You can also use it to compare the practice site pages that *you'll* create in Chapters 4 and 5 with the demo site's pages *we* have created. We are now going to continue building the **practice site**.

We suggest that you open the demo site in your *browser* now (i.e. *not* in PageBreeze), so that you can refer to it as you build the practice site.

1   In My Computer or Windows Explorer, browse to and double-click on the **DemoSite** folder in My Documents\My Webs to display all the files stored in that folder.

2   Double-click on the file named **index.htm**. (Your browser will open and display the home page of the demo site. By clicking on the links on the home page you can go to any of the other pages of the demo website without having to connect to the Internet, because it is stored on your hard drive.)

3   Back in My Computer or Windows Explorer, and My Webs, click on the folder named **Resources** to display its contents.

## BUILD THE PRACTICE SITE'S HOME PAGE

### Open the text document of page content

To make it easier for you, we've created a text document containing the content text for each of the pages in the practice site, so that instead of typing all the text into each page, you can simply copy and paste it from the text document.

The following screenshot shows the finished home page you're aiming to build. Refer back to this screenshot after you've completed each component, to check that you've achieved the desired result.

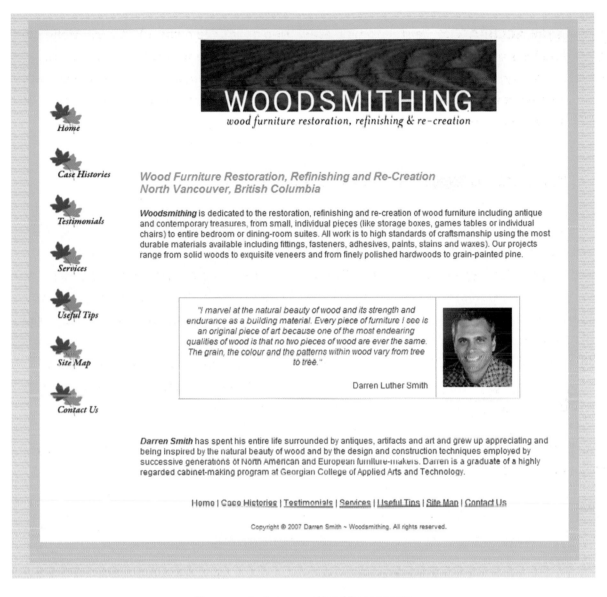

Demo website's completed home page

**WARNING: COPYING AND PASTING TEXT INTO WEB PAGES** Copying and pasting content from word processing programs (such as Microsoft Word or WordPad) is discouraged because the formatting of such programs merges with the formatting in your Web editor, often creating a mess. We strongly recommend that you use a plain text editing application such as NotePad (it comes bundled with Microsoft Windows) which does not create unnecessary code or formatting that can be carried into your Web page editor. When copying text from other websites or from Word documents, for pasting into any Web page editor, simply paste the copied text into NotePad first, which effectively cleans all the hidden formatting; then copy the cleaned text from NotePad and paste it into your Web page.

**1** In the Resources folder, double-click on the file named **TextContent.txt** and it will open in **NotePad**.

## Insert the page content

**1** With PageBreeze open at My Webs, double-click on the **Woodsmithing** folder and then, in the lower window, double-click on the file named **index.htm** (the home page of the practice website) to open it. (Make sure PageBreeze's **Normal** (edit) view tab is selected.)

**2** In the home page that opens, click to the right of the Woodsmithing banner and press `Enter` twice to position the cursor four lines beneath the banner.

**3** Click on the ≣ **Justify Left** Toolbar button to move the cursor to the left of the right-hand cell in the top row.

**4** Refer to the website blueprint document you put together during your initial planning stages, and type (don't copy and paste) the heading for your home page directly into the Web page in Normal view – for the practice site type **Wood Furniture Restoration, Refinishing and Re-Creation**.

**5** Press `Shift ⇧` + `Enter` to create a single line space beneath the heading you've just inserted.

**6** On that second line type **North Vancouver, British Columbia**.

**7** Restore the NotePad file **TextContent.txt** to view, and in it select and copy the first paragraph of text for the home page.

**8** Back in PageBreeze, click at the **end** of the line **British Columbia**, and press `Enter` to create a double line space and begin a new paragraph.

**9** Paste the copied text into the home page (two lines below the heading you typed).

**10** Press `Enter` twice to move down four lines and begin another new paragraph.

**11** Use the procedures in Chapter 4 (page 42) to insert a one-row, two-column nested table with these properties:
Width: **500 pixels**
Alignment: **Center**
Cell Padding: **10**
Border Size: **1**
Border color: **no border color**

**12** To insert the practice site's photo, click in the **right-hand cell** of the nested table to position the cursor there.

**13** On the Toolbar, click on the 🖻 **Insert Graphic** icon.

**14** In the **Insert Graphic** dialog box, double-click on the **images** folder in My Webs\Woodsmithing, and click on the file named **DarrenSmithPhoto.jpg** to select it.

**15** In the window under **Alternative Text**, type: **Darren Smith ~ Woodsmith**, and click on **OK**, then on 💾 **Save**.

**16** Refer again to the text document and copy the text to accompany the photo.

**17** In PageBreeze, click in the **left cell** of the nested table, and paste the text for the photo. (The cell will stretch to accommodate the text, and the other cell will shrink to fit the photo.)

**18** Click to the right of the outside of the nested table and press [Enter⏎] twice to start a new paragraph in the main content table and move down four lines.

**19** Copy and paste the remaining home page text from the NotePad file into the page.

**20** Format the heading text to change the colour, from the default brown to green, and to a larger size from the default 2 – for the practice site it is:
  • Font: already set at Arial, as the template default
  • Size: **4**
  • Style: **bold**, **italics**
  • Custom font colour: Red **145**, Green **156**, Blue **103**

**21** Format the content text:
  • The first words of each paragraph (***Woodsmithing*** and ***Darren Smith***) in bold italics
  • Inside the nested table:
    ○ Quotation: *italics*, not bold
    ○ Alignment: centre, then press [Enter⏎] for a new paragraph.
    ○ Darren's name: justify right, normal font (not italics)

**22** Save the changes.

**23** Click on the **Preview** tab to view the page as it would appear in Internet Explorer (see screenshot on page 55).

**24** Switch to your browser to view the demo version of the home page; compare our demo page with the practice page you've just created, and make any tweaks necessary to yours to make it the same as the demo page.

**25** To complete the page, click on the **Page Properties** tab and enter into the two Meta Tags windows the **Keywords** and the **Page Description** for the page. (For this practice page, copy and paste the home page's Meta Tags from the **ContentText.txt** NotePad file.)

---

### TIP: TO SEE THE DEMO PAGE IN PAGEBREEZE'S NORMAL VIEW

If you need to see the *structure* of the demo page: in PageBreeze's Normal view, double-click on My Webs to bring the **DemoSite folder** into view, then double-click the DemoSite folder and in the lower window, double-click on the **index.htm** file. To avoid confusion while working in PageBreeze, the demo pages all have the words DEMO SITE at the front of the page title as displayed in the blue PageBreeze Title bar. Always remember to check the page title before you start editing again, to make sure you're editing a *practice* site page and not a demo site page.

---

DEMO SITE Woodsmithing Wood Furniture Restoration - PageBreeze HTML Editor

File   Edit   View   Insert   Format   Table   Form   Tools   Help

---

### TIP:  HOW TO SEE THE PARAGRAPH AND LINE SPACING DETAILS

On the Menu bar, click on **View > Document Details**, and the paragraph and line spaces will be displayed. The little table beneath the next screenshot shows what each symbol means and how that line spacing is achieved.

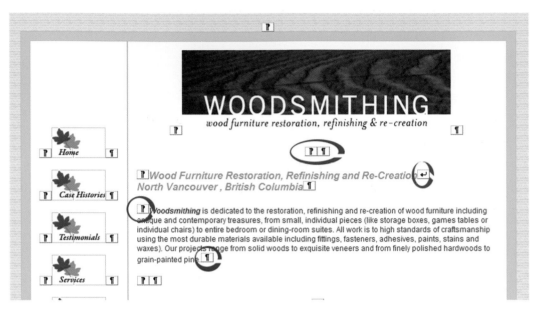

Paragraph and line spacing

| Symbol | Meaning | Created with |
|---|---|---|
| ↵ | Indicates a single line break; used to start a new line without beginning a new paragraph | Shift ⇧ + Enter ↵ |
| ¶ | Indicates the start of a new paragraph | Enter ↵ at the end of a paragraph |
| ¶ | Indicates the end of a paragraph | |
| ¶ ¶ | Indicates a paragraph break with no text in the paragraph | Enter ↵ |

---

### TIP: ALIGNMENT CHANGES

It's important to note that the paragraph end-mark ¶ (or *pilcrow*) holds all the formatting information for the paragraph just ended. If that paragraph is centred, then it's important to begin a new paragraph before you can start left-aligning or right-aligning new text.

## ADDING ADDITIONAL LINKS

A template, such as the one we created for the practice website, includes links that are common to the main pages of a website. These pages are often referred to as tier-one or level-one pages. Some of these pages may, however, link to tier-two pages (such as an image on a page of its own), where the linked destination is not accessible from the home page or from other tier-one pages. In such a case you'll need to create a new link from the particular tier-one page. Here is the procedure.

## Prepare the Web page

1 With PageBreeze in Normal view, open the file named **casehistories.htm** (in the Woodsmithing folder; also open the corresponding demo site page in your browser).

2 Follow the same procedures as for adding the content to the home page, only this time type **Case Histories** as the page heading. (Refer to page 57, step 20, to format this heading.)

3 Insert a one-row, two-column table for this page, and enter the table's properties:
   • Width: **100 Percent**
   • Cell Padding: **10**
   • Border: Size: **1**; Color: **no border colour**
   • Right-click inside the left cell of the table, and in **Row Properties**, set the Horizontal Alignment to **Center**.

4 Next, insert the two images from the **images** folder –
   in the left cell: **ChewedCouchArm.jpg**; in the right cell: **RepairedCouchArm.jpg**.

5 Restore the **TextContent.txt** NotePad file to view, and from it select and copy the text that describes the chewed arm.

6 Click to the right of the image in the left cell and press Enter.

7 Paste the copied text beneath the photo, and save the changes.

8 Follow the same procedure for pasting the applicable text beneath the photo on the right.

9 Click on the **Preview** tab, then switch to your browser window, and in the demo site page click on the **Case Histories** link to compare your practice page with ours.

10 To complete the page, click on the **Page Properties** tab and enter the page's Meta Tags text. (For this practice page, copy and paste the Case Histories page's Meta Tags from the **ContentText.txt** NotePad file.)

## Linking to an image file (in this case, a larger version of a photo)

1 Back in PageBreeze, on the Case Histories page, click on the photo of the repaired couch to select it, and click on the Toolbar's **Insert Hyperlink** icon.

2 Click in the **Local Document** radio button, then browse down to and double-click on the **images** folder in the top pane (screenshot next page).

3 Beneath the second pane, click on the **Show All File Types** check-box to display all the files in that folder.

4 Scroll down and click on the file named **CouchArmLarge.jpg** to select it.

5 Click on the little ⌄ **down** arrow next to the **Frame Target** box; click on **_blank** (to create a link that will open a separate browser window with the larger photo).

6 Click on **OK**; the dialog box will close and the small image on the Case Histories page will now link directly to the larger image in a separate window.

7 Save the page changes.

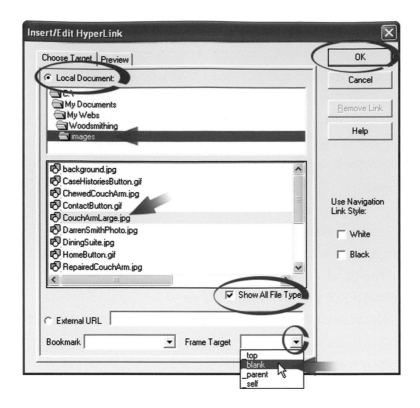

8   To test the link in PageBreeze, click on the **Preview (Internet Explorer)** tab to view the Case Histories page in browser format.

9   Click on the photo of the repaired couch arm and, if you did the procedure correctly, a new window will open showing only the larger photo of the repaired arm.

---

**NOTE: YOU CAN LINK TO VARIOUS DESTINATION TYPES**

You can use this same procedure to link to a second-tier Web page, an image, or even a specific place (called an *anchor* or *bookmark*) within the same page or in a different page.

---

## Linking to a different page

The previous procedure could also be used to link to a whole new page rather than just a larger photo. For example, you could create a Web page that holds several images on it, perhaps with accompanying text. Or you might want to explain something in more detail and have that explanation on a separate Web page.

To link to such a tier-two Web page, do this:

1   After clicking in the Local Document radio button in the previous procedure (step 2, page 59), browse to the website's folder and double-click on the appropriate **.htm** Web page that you might have created (e.g. **couchdetails.htm**); once the page has been saved, in Preview mode the hyperlink will then take you to that Web page.

## Linking to a place within a page (called an *Anchor* or *Bookmark*)

Sometimes a Web page needs to be scrolled down to view, for example, more detailed descriptions of different products or services, or a list of questions and answers. To avoid having the user scroll down and down to get to one particular item they wish to read, it is useful to have an itemized menu at the top of the page, with each menu item being a separate link to its particular topic on the same page. By clicking on a menu item, the hyperlink will take you directly to that topic. This is achieved by inserting what is known as an *anchor* or *bookmark*. We'll use the practice site's Useful Tips page to explain this.

1 From the text file **TextContent.txt**, select all the text for the **Useful Tips** page and copy it.

2 Back in PageBreeze (Normal view), in the **Woodsmithing** folder, double-click on the file **usefultips.htm** to open it in Normal view.

3 Click to the right of the banner and press `Enter ⏎` twice.

4 Click on the ☰ **Justify Left** Toolbar icon, then paste the copied text into the page.

5 Click at the end of the paragraph related to the heading CARING FOR YOUR WOOD FURNITURE and press `Enter ⏎`.

6 From the images folder, insert the graphic **DiningSuite.jpg** and centre it.

7 Click at the end of the paragraph related to the heading ANTIQUE WOOD FURNITURE and press `Enter ⏎`.

8 Insert the graphic **YellowHutch.jpg** and centre it.

9 Format the text according to the same **demo site** page, but do not underline the three topic headings or change their font colour to blue. (They are blue and underlined in the demo site page because they are hyperlinks, a step that will follow shortly for the practice page.)

10 To create the bookmarks that the hyperlinks will link to, click just in front of the following words: CARING FOR YOUR WOOD FURNITURE to position your cursor and indicate where you want to insert your first bookmark.

11 On the Menu bar, click on **Insert > Bookmark...**.

12 In the **Bookmark Name** window, type the name you want to give the bookmark – for this exercise, name it **caring** – and click on **OK** to close the Insert Bookmark dialog box.

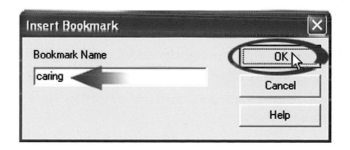

**13** Back on the practice Web page, select the text you want to link to that bookmark – the first topic heading *Caring for Wood Furniture* near the top of the page – and click on the Toolbar's **Insert Hyperlink** icon.

**14** In the dialog box that opens, click on:
- the **Local Document** radio button
- then on the **Show All File Types** check-box
- then on the **.htm page file** in which the bookmark has been created (**useful.tips** in this case)
- then on the **down arrow** at the **Bookmark** window
- then on the **name of the bookmark** you had created (**caring**)
- finally, on **OK**.

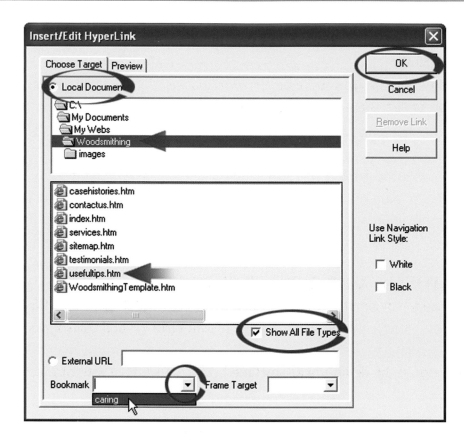

**15** Repeat steps 10 to 14 to insert the following bookmarks and hyperlinks too:
- Heading and link text: **Applying Wax to Wood Furniture**; bookmark name: **waxing**
- Heading and link text: **Antique Wood Furniture**; bookmark name: **antique**

**16** Save the changes.

**17** Click on the **Preview** tab and click on any one of the three **hyperlinked text headings** near the top, and its hyperlink will take you to the bookmarked topic heading lower down.

**NOTE: BOOKMARKS ON OTHER PAGES**

You can link to a bookmark on the same page, or to one inserted somewhere on a different page of your own website. If the bookmark is on a different page from where the link is located, clicking on the link will take you to the other Web page and to the specific bookmarked place on that page.

## Linking to a page on a different website

1   Follow the same procedures as above, but click on the radio button **External URL** instead.
2   Type in the full URL of the destination website after the **http://** (for example, type **www.reallyeasycomputerbooks.com**).

## Test the hyperlinks

It is essential that *every link* on your website be tested to make sure they're all working and there are no errors. (The Pro version of PageBreeze does this for you.)

1   Click on the **Preview (Internet Explorer)** tab.
2   Click on any hyperlinks you've created (on every page) and check that they do in fact take you to the required destination; if not, go back to Normal view and check for any errors that need to be fixed.

## EXPERIMENT WITH THE OTHER PRACTICE PAGES

We suggest that you use the other HTM pages to experiment with page, table and text formatting, adding and testing extra links, and so on, until you feel you're ready to start planning and building your own website.

In addition, you can refer to the demo site at any time by opening that in your browser as explained on page 54.

**TIP: DISSECT THE DEMO SITE PAGES**

If you really get stuck and need to examine how one of our demo pages has been set up, open it in PageBreeze's Normal view and check out the properties of the various elements making up the page, e.g. Page Properties, Backgrounds, Table/Cell/Row/Column Properties, Font Size, etc. If you *experiment* in a demo site page in any way, when you close the page and PageBreeze asks you whether you wish to save the changes, click on **No** – to ensure that the demo pages remain as we created them.

## SOME ADDITIONAL WEBSITE RESOURCES

There are various extra bells and whistles you can add to your site at any time, and several of them can be obtained free of charge from various Internet services. Here are a few pointers to help you.

### COUNTERS/TRACKERS

A tracker placed on your website helps you to see not only the number of people who have visited your site (called 'hits'), but with the right tracker you can also determine what countries your visitors came from, what browsers, operating systems, screen resolutions and screen colours they were using, which websites, e-mails or search engines referred them to you, and what keywords were used in any searches used.

This is all important information a Webmaster should know. These trackers are often available free of charge; but the price you pay is this: you must display the tracker icon on your webpage; they show only the statistics for one page of your site at a time; the stats are public for all to see, and there is advertising on your stats pages.

If you prefer a private tracker, there is likely to be a small monthly or yearly fee, but the benefits of paying for your tracker are that no one can see your stats except you; your stats pages are advert-free; there's unlimited multiple-page tracking; the tracker will tell you how long your visitors spent at your site, which pages they visited and how long they spent on each page, how they moved from page to page, exactly where they came from to get to your site, plus much more.

### Inserting a counter/tracker on a Web page

Once you've signed up for your tracker by submitting your site name, URL, password and login details, you will either be sent an email or be directed to another Web page where you would be given a very specific code to insert into your html.

1 In PageBreeze's Normal view, click where you wish to place your counter/tracker – usually at the bottom of your home page.

2 On the Menu bar, click on **Insert > HTML Code...** to open the **Insert HTML** dialog box.

3 Very carefully (so as to not change any of the line breaks) select and copy the script sent to you for the counter and paste it into the **HTML source:** window.

4 Click on **OK**; the counter icon should now be in its correct position on the page.

**NOTE: THE COUNTER IS LINKED TO THE SUPPLIER'S WEBSITE**

The counting and analysis of hits on your page is managed by the website offering the counter. To access this information (once your website is up and running online), click on the counter. If you're using a paid version, you will be supplied with a private URL where you can go and view your information after entering your password.

**Forms:** You can add various forms available from PageBreeze if you upgrade and pay for the PageBreeze Pro version. To see what forms are available, open a new page in PageBreeze and on the Menu bar click on *Form*. Insert some of the items that interest you, to get an idea of what they are. To make them usable, however, you need to subscribe to PageBreeze's Formbuilder service (which is available at no extra cost if you upgrade to PageBreeze Pro).

**Websites offering Webmaster tools:** Visit our companion website for links to suggested website services offering a variety of tools for Webmasters – for example: navigation buttons, background images, counters and trackers, other Web page editors, graphics editors, HTML scripts, auto-responders and much more.

**TIP: PROTECT YOUR E-MAIL ADDRESS AGAINST SPAM MAIL**

The way to insert an e-mail address on your Contact Us page is normally to create a hyperlink from text or an image. Instead of the hyperlink reading **http://www.etc**, it would read something like **mailto:darrensmith@woodsmithing.com** so that when someone clicks on your e-mail address, their e-mail client (e.g. Outlook Express) would open with a new message ready to be written. However, doing it this way would allow the spam robots to 'crawl' your site and harvest your e-mail address, and within a short while you would start receiving an increasing amount of unwanted spam (junk) mail. To avoid this, we suggest you 'cloak' your e-mail address so that it cannot be harvested by the spambots. We've provided a useful 'script' you can use to add this protection to any e-mail addresses you insert into your Web pages. You'll find the script in the file named **anti-spam.txt** which is stored on your computer in the **Resources** folder in My Webs.

## THE NEXT STEP

Once you've finished experimenting with the practice website, go back to the beginning of the book and work your way through chapters 1 through 5 again, and build your own website using the step-by-step procedures given to this point.

Once you've built your own website, and tested it thoroughly, you'll be ready to move on to Chapter 6 – publishing your site. This involves choosing a hosting service, registering your unique domain name and uploading all your files to the hosting server for final online testing and public access

# 6 Publishing your website

Once you're satisfied that your website is functioning properly and is ready to go 'live' for access by the general public around the world, it's time to arrange to have your site published on the World Wide Web. This involves three action steps:

1  Find a service provider to host your site (usually at an affordable monthly fee).
2  Register your own unique domain name (a reasonable registration fee with annual renewal).
3  Upload ('publish') all your website files to the hosting server (usually at no extra fee).

## FIND A SERVICE PROVIDER TO HOST YOUR SITE

When you register a domain name for your website you will need to provide the IP address of the Web server that will be hosting your site. Finding a service provider to host your site is therefore the first step to publishing your site, because it is this service provider who can give you the server address on which your domain will reside. They'll also be able to give you all the other details – ftp server's address, user name and password – that you'll need in order to upload your files to the server.

---

### CHOOSING A SERVICE PROVIDER

Before you start asking around in order to find a suitable hosting service provider, there are a few important things to consider, and you should know what they mean to you as a new Webmaster.

**Disk space:** This is the amount of space available on the hosting server for the storage of a client's file data; and it is measured in megabytes (MB). ISPs who provide clients with their normal Internet access typically include in their monthly fee some server space for hosting a personal website. This could be anything from 5 or 10 megabytes, perhaps even up to 20 MB; above this limit a hosting fee is payable. Companies specializing in website hosting usually charge a monthly hosting fee which is based on a sliding scale according to the amount of server space and other features required. You can get a feel of your own immediate needs by right-clicking on your website folder in My Webs, then clicking on Properties. The Properties dialog box will tell you the size of the entire folder contents. However, it's a good idea to allow for the likelihood that you'll want to add new pages and new content to your site over time. Remember too that having lots of high-quality photos and other images on your pages can consume a lot of disk space.

**Monthly transfer (bandwidth) limit:** Bandwidth refers to the amount of data that is transferred from the Web server to the Web browsers requesting to view Web pages on that server. It includes all the text and images on the requested page. Hosting service providers often set a monthly transfer or bandwidth limit, and this too can vary according to the fees payable. A small business site, without a great amount of traffic, would probably need about 2 gigabytes of bandwidth per month. If you've designed your site with good keywords to attract good traffic, then you'd most likely need more than this. So make sure your service provider has a plan whereby you can increase your bandwidth requirements as your site's popularity grows over time.

Also, check that whatever limit there is, it can be increased without a hassle. Some Web hosts set what is known as a hard limit, which means that if that limit is reached during the month, your entire site is shut down for the rest of that month. You can imagine how annoying that can be, to both you and your visitors. Also, when a site is shut down, for whatever reason, if Google happens to send their Googlebot out while your website is down, it is quite possible that you could lose your position in Google's rankings. So go for a service that either has no limit at all, or has a soft limit that can be increased mid-month if necessary.

**FTP access:** You need to be able to upload all the files for your entire site and then have access to your site whenever you need to update pages or add new pages to your site. This is vitally important if you wish to stay in control of your own site and avoid frustration and additional service fees. Also, choose a hosting service that does not charge you an extra fee every time you upload new files.

---

## Try your own Internet Service Provider (ISP) first

There are many hosting services available and it can be quite a challenge to decide who to choose as the host of your website. We therefore suggest that the quickest and easiest place to start would be your own Internet Service Provider through whom you have your normal access to the Internet. You've already made the decision to use them as your ISP, so you presumably feel quite comfortable with their level of competence. However, if there is any reason why you would prefer to use another ISP, then we'll also give you some tips about finding one (see the next item).

Use the following checklist when you contact your ISP – or any other providers – to enquire what they can offer you.

| | |
|---|---|
| ❏ | Do they offer server space for hosting a website? |
| ❏ | Is it included in the monthly fee you pay for Internet access? |
| ❏ | How much server space is offered free? (typically 5 to 10 MB) |
| ❏ | What are the charges for extra server space? |
| ❏ | Is there a bandwidth limit? If so, what is it? Monthly? |
| ❏ | Is any limit a *hard* limit, or is it a *soft* limit that won't shut down your site? |
| ❏ | Can you buy extra monthly bandwidth later? If so, at what fees? |
| ❏ | Is there any set-up fee? How much is it? |
| ❏ | Do they handle domain name registration? If so: |
| | ❏ What is the registration fee? |
| | ❏ What is the annual renewal fee? |
| | ❏ Does the registration make you the domain name owner? (essential) |
| ❏ | What other features are included in the hosting fee? |
| ❏ | What other optional features are offered, and at what extra fee? |
| | ❏ |
| | ❏ |
| | ❏ |
| | ❏ |
| | ❏ |
| | ❏ |
| ❏ | If you should later need to move your site to another hosting service, for whatever reason, does their service agreement allow that, and if so, is there any fee involved? |

## Finding alternative hosting services

If you don't want to use your existing ISP, here are some options you can try. Before you make a choice, remember to use the checklist already given.

❑ Type the following phrase into a search engine's Search window, including the quote marks: **'Web hosting services'** and visit any pages in the search results that look promising to you.

❑ To look for Web hosts in a particular country, add **+your country** at the end: e.g. **Web hosting services +Australia** (note: no space after the plus sign).

❑ Visit **http://www.hostingcatalog.com** and, as a start, click on a link to budget hosting and check out the various websites listed.

❑ Ask friends, colleagues and perhaps your local computer store gurus if they can recommend a hosting company, and why they recommend them.

❑ Finally, make the decision, knowing that you can always move your site to another host if you later find you're not happy with your existing one (sometimes at a fee, though).

# REGISTER YOUR DOMAIN NAME

### WHAT'S IN A NAME?

A URL is the unique address of a website and includes the user's domain name (e.g. *woodsmithing* for our practice site) combined with a top-level domain that denotes other characteristics of the site, such as a commercial site (**.com** or **.co**), a non-profit organization (**.org**), a government site (**.gov**), etc., and often the country as well (e.g. the United Kingdom's **.uk**, Australia's **.au**, South Africa's **.za**, New Zealand's **.nz**, Canada's **.ca** and so on). For example, **www.woodsmithing.co.uk** would indicate:

- the user's unique domain name *woodsmithing*
- the top-level domain **.co**, indicating that it is a commercial website
- the country domain abbreviation, **.uk** for the United Kingdom

Note that the *full domain* format is actually what is registered, so there might be a domain registered by someone in Australia, www.woodsmithing.co.au, another owned by someone in the USA, www.woodsmithing.com, another anywhere else, www.woodsmithing.biz. In order to protect all popular variations of a particular name, some companies will spend a lot of money to register many versions of the same core name. However, for budgetary reasons, most individuals don't take it that far. Note too that you do not need to register a country-specific domain name, nor are you prohibited from registering any kind of top-level domain you feel is appropriate for your site. For example, if you live in the UK and want to have an international flavour to your domain name, then you can still register a **.com** domain name if you so wish.

You can learn a lot about how the domain name register works by visiting the website of the Internet Corporation for Assigned Names and Numbers (ICANN) at **http://www.icann.org**, and in particular their list of Accredited Registrars. This gives a complete list of all the companies authorized to register a domain name, and the specific top-level domains they are authorized to allocate. The list is available at **http://www.icann.org/registrars/accredited-list.html**.

## First check with your ISP or hosting service

The provider of your Web hosting server space will usually be able to register a domain name for you too. However, you'll need to tell them what domain name you want registered. And if you want them to do all the checking to see if that name is available, then you'll probably need to give them a second and a third choice as well, in case your first choice has already been registered by someone else. Ask your service provider what their requirements are, and also the costs (registration fee and annual renewal fee).

If you wish, you can do some preliminary searching yourself to see if your preferred domain name is available; and you can even handle your own registration. However, we suggest that beginners should rather let their ISP handle it for them.

---

**TIP: YOU'LL NEED TWO DNS IP NUMBERS TO REGISTER A DOMAIN NAME**

If you register a domain name yourself, you'll need to ask your hosting service for their DNS (domain name server) information. This will be two numbers; *Primary* (e.g. 66.241.145.145) and *Secondary*: (e.g. 66.241.146.146).

---

## UPLOAD YOUR FILES TO THE HOSTING SERVER

Finally the great moment has arrived. It's time to upload all your website files to the hosting server and go 'live' for the public to see your new presence on the World Wide Web. The process you'll use to do this is called File Transfer Protocol (FTP) which you'll do by means of an FTP program.

---

**FTP CLIENTS**

Many of the good Web page authoring programs, such as HotDog, Expression Web and Dreamweaver, have an FTP client built into them. (PageBreeze has one in its Pro version.) There are also stand-alone FTP clients such as the popular WS_FTP, available from **http://www.ipcwitch.com**, where you can download either the Home or the Pro version for a 30-day free trial. For this tutorial we'll be using an easy-to-use freebie we found on the Web, called FTP Commander.

---

## Install and open the FTP Commander software

1  In My Webs\Programs, double-click on the **commanderftp.exe** file to install the **FTP Commander** software for the next procedures.
2  Open **FTP Commander** on your screen and notice the layout of the window (see next page).

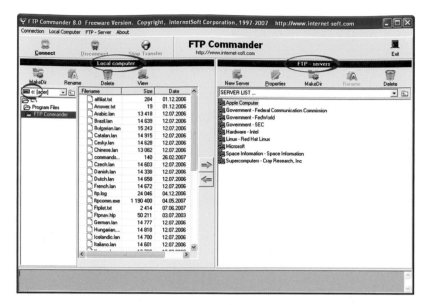

The drives, folders and files on your own computer are displayed in the left-hand **Local computer** window. The files listed in the middle pane are the files inside the FTP Commander folder; you can ignore them for now. A list of FTP servers is shown in the right-hand **FTP - servers** window; you can ignore those too.

## Add your hosting server to the server list

In order to upload your files to the hosting server, you need to configure the FTP client so that it can find and connect to the server. For this, you need the FTP Server Name, User ID and Password given to you by the service provider who will be hosting your website.

---

1    In the **FTP - servers** window, click on the **New Server** button on the left, to open the **FTP Server Properties** window.

---

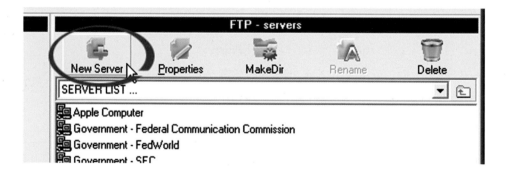

---

2    Have the **FTP details** at hand, as given to you by your hosting service provider.

3    In the various text windows in the upper half of the **FTP Server Properties** window, accurately type the following:

     • **Name** – your domain name (or some other name that you will recognize as being the server on which your website will be hosted). For our practice site we've entered the name Telus - Woodsmithing.

     • **FTP Server** – the ftp address (we've used **ftp.telus.net** as an example).

---

- **FTP Port** – usually 21; so leave this unchanged, unless your service provider has advised otherwise.
- **User ID** – as advised by your service provider (no more than eight characters).
- **Password** – as advised by your service provider.

**4**  Make sure that all three of the check-boxes below the Password box have a tick in them; if not, click in each one to add a tick. (If you want your password visible, uncheck **Mask Password**.)

**5**  When done, click on **Save**; FTP Commander is now configured to be able to access your hosting server when you click on Connect (later).

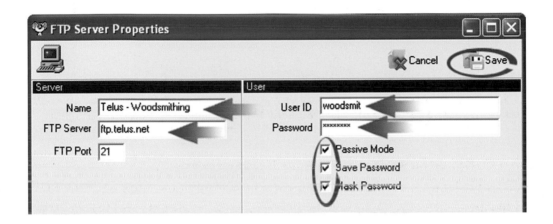

**NOTE: CONFIGURING OTHER FTP CLIENTS**

Most FTP clients can be set up in much the same way as explained here for FTP Commander.

**TIP: YOU CAN RENAME OR DELETE A LISTED SERVER**

If you want to rename the server from what you've called it, simply right-click on the name, then click on **Server Properties** and type in the new name. To delete the server configuration altogether (e.g. if you later change to a different service provider and will no longer be using the existing FTP address), right-click on the server name in the menu shown on the right, and click on **Delete Server/Dir/File**. In the confirmation box that opens, click on **Yes**.

## Browse to the files you'll upload

Before you connect to the server, browse to display the files you'll upload in order to have them ready for uploading.

> **1** In the left-hand pane of the **Local computer** window, double-click the **C:\** drive (see screenshot below left) to view the other folders on your C:\ drive.
>
> **2** Browse to and double-click on the folder containing all your new website files (see screenshot below right for the practice site example).

 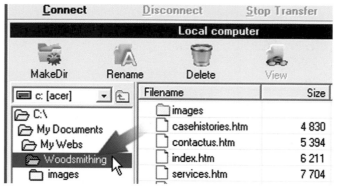

## Connect to the server and upload the files

> **1** In the **FTP – servers** pane, click on the name you gave your server (screenshot below left shows our practice site example).
>
> **2** On the **Menu** bar, click on the **Connect** icon (screenshot below right); FTP Commander will now start connecting to the hosting server. (You can also connect by double-clicking on the server name.)

 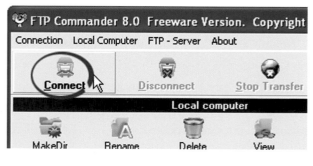

The connection status is always displayed in the lower panel of FTP Commander:

Once you're connected to the server, your User ID will be displayed in the window on the right.

**3** Hold down the [Shift] key, and in the **Local computer** window click on the **first folder/file** you want to upload, and then on the **last one**, and all the files will be selected and highlighted; release the [Shift] key; be sure to select the **images** folder too. (The total size and number of files selected will be displayed below the file list.)

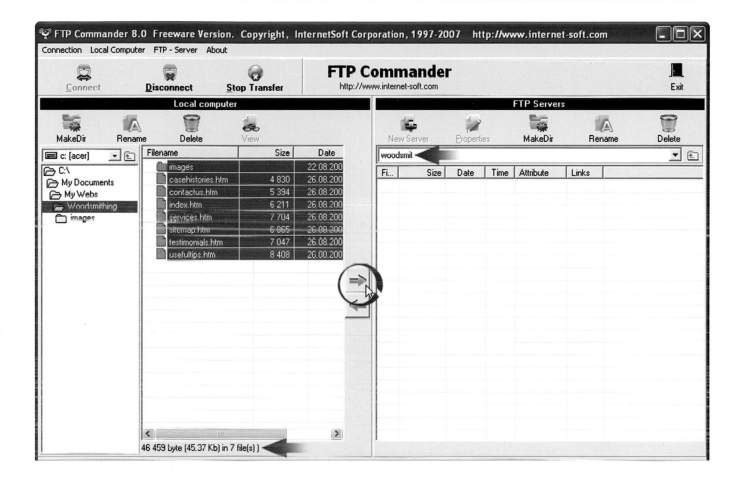

**4** Click on the right-pointing **Upload** arrow located between the two windows (see screenshot above), to start uploading all the files to the remote server; a progress box will display the file upload status (screenshot on next page).

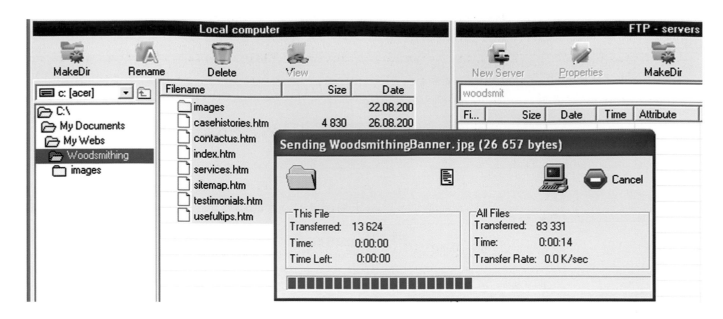

Once the upload has been completed, the right-hand window will display all the files now stored on the hosting server. Your website is now active on the World Wide Web for all to access.

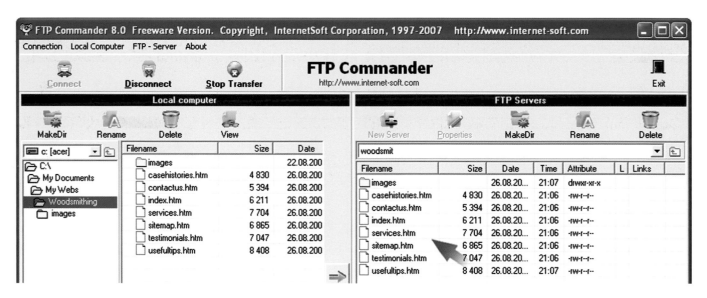

**TIP: TO DELETE A FILE FROM THE SERVER**

If you need to delete a file from the server, simply click on the file name in the FTP Servers window and on the Toolbar click on the **Delete** icon.

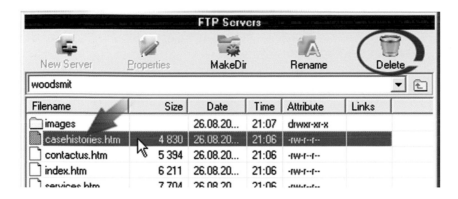

**5** Once all the files have been uploaded, click on the **Disconnect** Toolbar button to disconnect from the remote server.

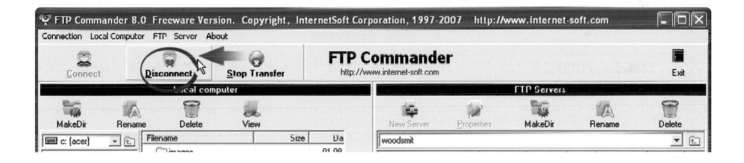

## TEST YOUR ONLINE WEBSITE IMMEDIATELY

Once your website is online it can be visited by anyone from anywhere in the world. It can also be crawled by search engine robots and added to their databases. So, even though you should have previewed your website in one or two browsers before you uploaded it to the server, it is very important to open your primary Internet browser as well as your secondary browsers and check your online site yourself to make sure everything is working as you had intended. Here's a checklist of what to look for. (Check your site on a Mac computer too, if you have access to one.)

### Website functionality checklist

❏ Are all the images displayed in their correct positions?

❏ Are all the menu buttons (if you've used images) also correctly displayed?

❏ Test every link: does it take you to the page it should take you to?

❏ Do all the fonts look correct, as you had designed the page on your computer?

❏ Does the background appear as you wanted it to look?

❏ Repeat the above checks on every single page on your site.

### Fix any errors as soon as possible

1  Make a note of every error you find on every page.

2  Go to your website files that are stored on your hard drive in the folder **My Webs**, open PageBreeze and on each Web page fix each error, and save the file again.

3  Once you've fixed all the errors, load FTP Commander again, connect to the hosting server and upload those amended files as before. (The new files will automatically replace the older versions on the server.)

4  Disconnect from the server.

5  In your Internet browser click on the **Refresh** button to clear the earlier versions of your Web pages you visited, and visit your website again.

6  Check every page online again; if you find more errors, repeat these steps.

 **REFRESH YOUR BROWSER WINDOW** Whenever you've viewed a Web page, and changes have since been made, before viewing it again make sure you refresh the entire website by pressing the keyboard's Shift⇧ key while clicking on the Refresh button in the browser. Even better: delete the temporary Internet files in your cache.

## Congratulations, and all the best!

# Our thanks to

**Darren Luther Smith ~ Woodsmith**
for permission to use his website at
**www.woodsmithing.com**
as the basis for the mini-version that we created
specially for use in the tutorials of this book

# and our acknowledgements to

the various suppliers of the freeware programs
we have had the opportunity to promote by means of
this educational publication, specifically:

**PageBreeze at www.pagebreeze.com**
(PageBreeze Web page editor)

**Softnik Strategic Software at www.softnik.com**
(Good Keywords and Keyword Explorer)

**Irfanview at www.irfanview.com**
(Irfanview graphic viewer)

**Adobe at www.adobe.com**
(Adobe Reader for reading PDF files)

**InternetSoft Corporation at www.internet-soft.com**
(FTP Commander ftp client)

# INDEX

Reprinted in 2009
First published in 2008 by
New Holland Publishers (UK) Ltd
London · Cape Town · Sydney · Auckland

Garfield House
86–88 Edgware Road
London, W2 2EA
United Kingdom
www.newhollandpublishers.com

80 McKenzie Street
Cape Town 8001
South Africa

Unit 1, 66 Gibbes Street
Chatswood, NSW 2067
Australia

218 Lake Road
Northcote, Auckland
New Zealand

Copyright © 2008 text: Gavin Hoole and Cheryl Smith
Copyright © 2008 photographs and illustrations: Cheryl Smith
Copyright © 2008 design and presentation: Gavin Hoole
Copyright © 2008 New Holland Publishers (UK) Ltd

All rights reserved. No part of this publication may be reproduced,
stored in a retrieval system, or transmitted in any form or by any means,
electronic, mechanical, photocopying, recording or otherwise,
without the prior written permission of the publishers and copyright holders.

3 5 7 9 10 8 6 4 2

ISBN 978 1 84773 073 2

Editor: Amy Corbett
Design: AG&G Books
Production: Laurence Poos
Editorial Direction: Rosemary Wilkinson

Reproduction by Pica Digital PTE Ltd, Singapore
Printed and bound by Times Offset, Malaysia